# ANOINTED PREACHING:
## The Holy Spirit and the Pulpit

*Bryan Norford*

**Bryan Norford**

The Pebble Press
Lethbridge Canada
www.pebblepress.ca

ANOINTED PREACHING
The Holy Spirit and the Pulpit

Copyright © 2011 Bryan Norford

All rights reserved. No part of this publication may be reproduced, stored in a retrieval system, or transmitted in any form or by any means—electronic, mechanical, photocopy, recording, or any other—except for brief quotations in printed reviews, without prior permission from the publisher.

All Scripture references are taken from the Holy Bible, New International Version, Copyright © 1973, 1978, 1984 by the International Bible Society. Used by permission of Zondervan Publishing House.

ISBN-10: 146378080X
ISBN-13: 978-1463780807

The Pebble Press
pebblepress.ca

## DEDICATION

*This book honours my beloved parents, Adelaide and Francis Norford, who found Christ in the pentecostal tradition, nurtured me in the Christian faith, and sustained their own faith to the end*

Other books by Bryan Norford:

*Happy Together: Daily insight from Families from Scripture*
    (with Ann Norford)
*Guess who's Coming to Reign: Jesus Talks about His Return*
*Gone with the Spirit: Tracking the Holy Spirit through the Bible.*

# CONTENTS

**PREFACE** ........................................................................... 1

**INTRODUCTION** ............................................................. 5

**1: THE EXPERIENCE OF SPIRIT ANOINTED PREACHING** ... 11
    The Understanding of Anointed Preaching
    The Experience of Spirit Anointing on Preparation
    The Experience of Spirit Anointing on Delivery
    Summary

**2. THE THEOLOGICAL BASIS FOR ANOINTED PREACHING** ... 33
    The Relationship of Hermeneutics to Preaching
    The Scriptural Pattern of Anointing
    Pentecostal Trends in Hermeneutics
    Summary

**3. THE NEED FOR INTEGRITY AND FLEXIBILITY** ... 53
    The Content and Purpose of Anointed Preaching
    The Need for Flexibility of Sermon Style
    A Review of Traditional Pentecostal Styles
    Summary

## 4. THE SIGNS OF ANOINTED PREACHING     71
    The Need for Experience
    The Experience of Signs Following
    The Paradox of Power: Its Foundation of Weakness
    The Sign of the Fruit of the Spirit
    Summary

## CONCLUSION     93

## APPENDICES     97
    1. A Review of the Scriptural Significance of Anointing
    2. New Testament View of the Holy Spirit as Communicator
    3. The Necessity of Weakness in the New Testament
    4. Some Outlines of Pentecostal Sermons

## BIBLIOGRAPHY     125

# PREFACE

This preface is really a postscript. The original script for this book was written about 1992 for a Regent College thesis that was never completed. Thus apart from some editing and minor updating, time related material is a couple of decades old. However, the principles discussed are timeless, so are still relevant and worth consideration.

In my view, the Pentecostal Church has continued to mature during the last twenty years to the point where it is closer to its evangelical brethren in its education and service format. In fact, much of what I wrote in the conclusion is evident today. This is particularly true of the larger churches, where logistics make audience participation in the verbal gifts of the Spirit more difficult. Under these conditions, small groups allow use of those gifts where participation is more natural. In smaller churches, fewer numbers allow participation in verbal gifts during more formal services.

Preaching has been affected also, but it is a two way street. The charismatic movement has infiltrated to some degree into most conservative denominations; the understanding of the Spirit's work in preaching is far more recognized and accepted. Thus, the gap between Pentecostals and Evangelicals has narrowed from both sides. Has this had an effect of reducing the "fire" in pentecostal preaching? This varies from church to church, but I believe increasing maturity has increased the sense of humility into the boldness of Holy Spirit delivery.

Thus, the Pentecostal Church has become more of the accepted core, rather than the fringe radical at its inception. However, there is the looming danger that the freer fellowships and independent churches may fall prey to recent radical reader-response theories of hermeneutics. Here, the text is received as a "floating" document, not moored to the author's intention, but available to be towed in any direction the reader thinks fit.

This, of course, allows for any fanciful interpretation the reader wishes or needs to make. Already, the Canadian Charter of Rights and Freedoms has fallen prey to this idea, courts inserting meaning not intended by its original framers. According to Chief Justice McLaughlin, the Charter is a "living tree" that needs to conform to changing cultural values. This type of understanding of texts, divorced from their historical moorings, is naturally amenable to a postmodern society.

Unfortunately, the basic problem that has plagued Pentecostals, that of seeking personal Spirit enlightenment rather than biblical knowledge, has followed the Charismatic into the wider Christian community. The resulting biblical illiteracy is fertile soil for reader-response approach. That, in turn, may foster abuse of spiritual gifts for personal needs and promotion, a hindrance to congregational maturity. This is in opposition to the intended role of the Holy Spirit to provide power to "be my witnesses . . . to the ends of the earth, Acts 1:8."

Whatever the future role of the pentecostal and charismatic movements, there will always be challenges for the Christian community to overcome. But in recent travels, I was encouraged by the numerous large churches, both pentecostal and evangelical in cities and towns across Canada. Increasing faithfulness to the word in pentecostal preaching and a greater awareness of the empowering of the Spirit in preaching in other fellowships can only improve understanding of the Gospel. Not only will congregations increase in spiritual maturity, but the witness of the

## Anointed Preaching

Holy Spirit will draw the prevailing culture to the truth of the Gospel.

Bryan Norford, Lethbridge, Canada, 2011

Bryan Norford

# INTRODUCTION

This book seeks authentic signs of the Holy Spirit's work in preaching, with particular emphasis on the tradition of the Pentecostal Church. Traditionally labelled "the anointing," the enthusiasm of early pentecostal preaching in both zeal and passion was real. Many were attracted to the pentecostal freedom of worship, the joy, fervour, and depth of conviction of adherents, and the emphasis on lay involvement—both encouraged by the leadership, claimed by the pew, and typified by the preaching.

Whatever discussion there may be on the finer points of pentecostal theology, and despite whatever misinformation or even abuse it may have brought about, the emphasis on the need of the Holy Spirit to convey the truth of the Gospel has not been given its scriptural weight in other fellowships. Apart from lip service, parameters of the Holy Spirit's work in preaching have been largely ignored in most books on preaching. Typical are the major works on preaching by Sturtevant, Broadus and Grady Davis who ignore the topic. Those popular writers on preaching, Daniel Baumann and Martyn Lloyd-Jones, who take time to emphasize the Spirit's role, generally see it as a mysterious, subjective topic generally unsuitable for close scrutiny.

In recent years, some, from curiosity or thirst, have waded into the murky water of Spirit anointed preaching to find if a living spring still feeds it! This book draws together threads of some attempts to define more clearly the Spirit's anointing role in preaching. If Pentecostals can express a valid theological base for the Spirit's role in preaching, a genuine recovery of earlier dynamic is possible, without losing a century of cultural development. The Spirit's role here is not the prerogative of the Pentecostal; his work is primary in all Christian witness. If the Spirit's work in preaching is, as I believe, the core and life of the preacher's commission and ability to proclaim the Gospel, it is a major area of reflection needed within the overall doctrine of preaching, even beyond the limits of pentecostal dialogue.

The causes of energetic ministry may be with or without the Spirit's influence. There is always the possibility of a move away from dependence on God and his Spirit towards self-reliance and control. Lack of clear guidance, or even inaccurate teaching on what authenticates the work of the Spirit, has created an audience for the divergent and congregations led by enthusiastic, but frequently uninspired (in the theological sense), and unbiblical "preaching."

However, while the experiential sense of the Holy Spirit's unction in preaching, both inside and outside the pentecostal movements, has been clearly documented, the scriptural underpinnings have not. Thus, misconception concerning "anointed preaching" has arisen outside the pentecostal movement, and needs validating clarity. Anointed preaching has been characterized a number of ways, but for our purpose can be summarized as "preaching beyond ourselves," described and defined in more detail in chapter one. The emphasis on the need of the Spirit generally has been a cornerstone of the pentecostal movement, particularly in preaching. But the experience is not limited to Pentecostals; and we note many cases of other notable preachers who testify to this experience.

Anointed preaching must begin with hermeneutics, in our case, particularly the hermeneutics that determine the preacher's interpretation of the word to a particular audience—the hermeneutics of the pulpit. Accurate preaching depends not only on an accurate understanding of the word that inspires it, but also on recognizing the Spirit's freedom in the work of preaching.

Thus, chapter two seeks to apply a widened scope of hermeneutics desired by Pentecostals for preaching, on the basis that the word without the Spirit is dead. Yet in practice, if not admitted, many pentecostal-type preachers imply that the Spirit operates without the word. There is always a danger that "freedom" in the Spirit can slide from freedom *in* the word to freedom *from* the word.

Despite efforts within the movement to impose a format of preaching on Pentecostals, they continue to use a variety of styles of preaching, some questionable to many. This flexibility has led on occasion to lack of focus and dubious motivation for some pentecostal preaching. A maturing pentecostal movement cannot afford to return simply to the good old days and times of ignorance that God may have winked at. Any return to the essence of Pentecostalism—its dependence on the Spirit of power—must be in today's context. The high level of today's evangelical scholarship cannot be ignored with integrity and must be incorporated into today's pentecostal preaching, so an *accurate* Gospel may be proclaimed in power. Yet style is less important than content which remains constant—the Gospel of Jesus Christ. Chapter three calls for flexibility in style, while retaining the central content and purpose of preaching the gospel.

I believe intensely the whole counsel of God and its liberating message will attract and mould secure, strong individuals. This belief is strengthened by the knowledge that the Holy Spirit illumines and convicts of the truth of the message and he gives power for witness to it. That combination which gave the pentecostal movement its original fire can do so again. It was care and compassion for this movement that brought me to faith. It prompts my optimism for its future; that the dangers lurking in the movement may be recognized and, unlike Samson, the potential departure of the Spirit recognized before it is too late. While there may be many areas of evidence to be explored, and while the final evidence of the Spirit's work may be more clearly seen over time, I want to explore short term remedies that may address the dilemma.

Thus chapter four reviews the content, demeanour and delivery, and how listeners can safeguard themselves, and ensure growth toward Christian maturity. Misreading the immediate signs following delivery can be a hindrance, if not disastrous, for the hearer. Scripture may be used as an excuse for the dissemination of personal agendas, and "crediting" the Holy Spirit with the result based on "signs following."

Although "signs following" are generally scripturally based, they are not infallible. For instance, Jesus used signs to authenticate his message, yet warns that some operate in his name with signs following who are bogus. Chapter four also calls for a greater awareness of the fruit of the Spirit in the life of the preacher as a guide to authenticity.

This search has its pitfalls. Discernment itself is a gift of the Spirit, and who can discern the discerning work of the Spirit? And of even greater concern is the attempt to define the working of a sovereign Spirit. To provide guidelines to recognize him may simply straight-jacket him for our purposes. We are always in danger of understanding in order to control. Yet as Scripture gives clear guidelines for safeguarding the Church against the spurious, so we need to find guidance for the serious work of "anointed preaching."

Finally, let me clarify some definitions for some terminology used.

"Anointed preaching" refers to the empowering work of the Holy Spirit in preaching, as demonstrated by Jesus and displayed by the apostles, whether consciously experienced or not, and will not refer to the commonly held misunderstanding with regard to style unless stated.

"Enduement" and "unction" are frequently used to describe the Holy Spirit's empowering activity, again whether consciously experienced or not, and will be used with the same meaning.

"Pentecostal" will refer to pentecostal denominations generally, although much of the subject matter will be also relevant to the charismatic movement.

Bryan Norford

# 1

## THE EXPERIENCE OF SPIRIT ANOINTED PREACHING

> *"The Spirit of the Lord is on me, because he has anointed me to preach good news to the poor. He has sent me to proclaim freedom for the prisoners and recovery of sight to the blind, to release the oppressed, to proclaim the year of the Lord's favour."*
>
> Luke 4:18–19

Discussion of the anointing of the Spirit in preaching is hampered by a variety of misunderstandings related to its definition. In my view, these have also caused some of the problems that the Pentecostal Churches currently face. This chapter reviews the varied understanding of anointed preaching, current related problems and solutions being practised, and attempts to better define the idea of anointed preaching. Most views of the anointing are based on experience, although a scriptural basis is available and is discussed in chapter two. This chapter will also document widespread recorded experiences of anointing on both preparation and delivery.

# THE UNDERSTANDING OF ANOINTED PREACHING

## The Popular Understanding

What are the marks of the "Spirit anointed" preacher? There is no doubt that the signs are widely misunderstood; certainly by listeners, or there would be no congregation for the inauthentic! But tragically it seems that many preachers themselves are either misguided, or deliberately misleading on this issue. It is too easy to use even God-given gifts in a natural way to achieve desired results. Martyn Lloyd-Jones, possibly unconsciously, reveals the problem in his book, *Preachers and Preaching*.

In the first chapter he gives the scornful title of "pulpiteers" to those who command the pulpit and sway crowds by their force of personality or oratory, but could never be called "preachers" in the scriptural sense.[1] Yet in the last chapter of the same book he describes what he calls the Spirit's "unction," or the influence of the Holy Spirit in his own preaching.[2] He admits failure to define this unction, beyond its liberating experience, and certainly fails in that chapter to indicate guidelines for assessing the difference between the "enthusiasm" of the pulpiteer and the "Spirit anointed" preacher, and to provide some guidelines for discerning which Spirit (spirit) is in the pulpit.

Thus, we need to review the generally understood meaning of anointed preaching if we are to understand how problems arise in pentecostal preaching. The popular understanding continues to flourish because there is no doctrinal position articulated by the movements, and congregations have come to accept and expect substandard preaching that goes by that name. Any accepted understanding is that which has arisen from pentecostal literature on preaching (documented later), gained mainly from experience. Thus, it is the common understanding held by congregations,

---

[1] D. Martyn Lloyd-Jones, *Preaching and Preachers*. (Grand Rapids MI: Zondervan Publishing House, 1971), 13–15.

[2] Lloyd-Jones, *Preaching and Preachers*, 304–325.

## Anointed Preaching

which has caused deterioration in pentecostal preaching, as pastors attempt to conform to a pattern established among Pentecostals at large. This view of "the anointing" which grew up ad hoc over the life of Pentecostalism needs to be addressed.

The pentecostal understanding of the operation of the Holy Spirit in preaching has resulted in a distinctive style—assured, intense, passionate, "fire-in-the-bones" type of delivery. It stresses the Holy Spirit, audience participation, and is frequently long and extemporary. It will usually call for a response to the message preached by a call to the altar with "signs following."

These are general characteristics, and not to be discarded on that basis alone. But all too frequently, the more of the above, the more likely the label of "anointed preaching" will be given to it. The style has become normal for many audiences, and the "spiritual" content of the message measured by the passion, emotion, and decibel level of delivery and response, more often than the biblical content of the message.

**Current Problems in Pentecostal Preaching**

Lack of a clear understanding of anointed preaching has resulted in segments of the present movement losing the reality for the form. Form was, of course, the avowed anathema of Spirit directed worship, yet emptiness is apparent in much pentecostal preaching. As one disgruntled preacher put it:

> Some suggest that preaching is outdated and ineffective—hence a move to replace the sermon with discussion groups, chats on sociological problems, entertainment, dialogue, drama, and social action. The quality of preaching has also suffered. Laziness has set in with some pastors buying ready-made sermons. This is unacceptable, and far removed from the work of the Spirit in guiding, inspiring and directing the preacher.[1]

---

[1] Roger Woods, "Preach the Word," *Resource*, 5:2, (November-December

Probably related to this, the growth of the movement is slowing. There is a noticeable drift by people from pentecostal churches in Canada to other evangelical churches with little compensating reverse movement. Thomas Miller states that scores of people moving out of a large pentecostal church complained of either "dead" worship or "too little Bible" in the preaching.[1] Many of my personal friends and family have made this move despite roots in the movement either by natural or spiritual birth. The usual reason given is lack of either sustaining content or spiritual integrity—in my view the former is the cause of the latter. Thus, because of conformity to an empty form of preaching, often with little relation to the Scriptures that give it meaning, many existing pentecostal churches are struggling to stay alive with dwindling congregations, internal squabbling and superficial, insecure Christian experience.

**Some Current Solutions**
There is no shortage of reasons given for this state. The most common reason claimed is the loss of traditional pentecostal roots and this has prompted a return to more emphasis on pentecostal distinctives—generally characterized by the traditional baptism of the Holy Spirit and greater use of the vocal gifts of the Spirit in worship. This includes the desire for a return to *more* "anointed" preaching. Much of this reasoning is coupled with an anti-intellectual stance, where education is considered a "faulty proposal" to make the Gospel more effective.[2] It is rather the anointing that brings blessing:

---

1990) 11.
[1] Thomas W. Miller, "O Foolish Pentecostals," *The Pentecostal Testimony*, (October 1991), 30.
[2] Thomas W. Miller, "O Foolish Pentecostals," 28, where he sarcastically quotes as one of several "faulty proposals" from PAOC publications: "The academics in the PAOC will lead the way into a future which thus will be more rewarding and respectable."

## Anointed Preaching

It would, in these days, be foolish to ignore scholastic achievement. In the realm of commerce, medicine, and numerous other fields, knowledge can be a tremendous asset. However, in the field of spiritual things and the need to effectively present the glorious message of the risen Christ, our success depends solely on the anointing of the Holy Spirit.[1]

On this basis, it appears that more of what is responsible for decline will be the cure!

As an opposite reaction to this dilemma, some pentecostal teachers of homiletics are using accepted evangelical texts and verbally admit to discouraging students from traditional "pentecostal preaching." Gary Smalley sees a slow change in pentecostal preaching:

> There is less of Jimmy Swaggart, and more of Charles Swindoll. Of course, what we lacked in depth we made up in length! Much of the movement and volume which accompanied the shallow content of many an early pentecostal sermon are now replaced by well-constructed messages showing respect for the needs and intellects of the people in the pew. Some will say that passion is lacking in pentecostal preaching today, and they have a point. But today, preachers are communicating better. It used to be that traditional Pentecostals were easily aroused by the spit and polish of the orator/evangelist who downgraded education in favour of some immediate revelation which made study and preparation unnecessary. This is slowly changing. The new pentecostal minister is aware of the danger of an extra-biblical, emotion-centred theology.[2]

---

[1] Ron Reid, "Academic or Anointed?" *The Pentecostal Testimony*, January 1986.

[2] Gary E. Smalley, "Anticipating Not a Decade of Disaster, But . . . ," *The*

The change is to be welcomed, yet the movement will lose much of its character and drive if the idea of anointed preaching is lost. To opt for a total evangelical method and style may be throwing out the baby with the bathwater.

## A Proposed Understanding
As Pentecostals and Charismatics have played a significant role in the renewing of the Church, so there should be a place for their traditional style of preaching. Perhaps because the concept of anointed preaching subconsciously carries with it much of the exuberance, even excess that has often characterized charismatic preaching, the subject has been avoided by evangelical scholarship as aberrant, and prevailing assumptions have, for the most part, gone unchallenged. Thus a continuing serious look at the scriptural implications for anointed preaching, the precedent for which was set by Jesus himself is needed. The anointing of the Holy Spirit was necessary for Jesus to convey the Gospel in word and deed,[1] the Holy Spirit was sent by Jesus to bring conviction of the truth of the Gospel,[2] and Jesus taught the power of the Spirit was necessary for propagation of the Gospel by his followers.[3]

While we seek a validation of anointed preaching, we cannot validate current ideas wholesale. We recognize a basic truth in the concept, that of "preaching beyond ourselves," but which has become distorted by blurred understanding and casual practice. Therefore, the following two ideas should be included in the concept of "preaching beyond ourselves," but are at variance with commonly accepted pentecostal ideas of anointed preaching.

First, anointed preaching is a broader concept than the simple act of preaching. Anointing of the preacher has to do with the call of a preacher, as well as empowering for the individual sermon. Second, anointed preaching, while mainly recognized by

---

*Pentecostal Testimony*, March 1990, 16.
[1] Luke 4:18-19.
[2] John 16:8ff.
[3] Acts 1:8.

Pentecostals, is not restricted to them. Non-Pentecostals have experiences similar to the pentecostal idea of anointing; a difficult area for those pentecostals who hold that the anointing is dependent on Spirit-baptism, for in their view, those who do not claim the experience of Spirit-baptism cannot be anointed for preaching.

## THE EXPERIENCE OF SPIRIT ANOINTING ON PREPARATION

The on-going sense of anointing upon both preparation and delivery is a necessary part of the pentecostal tradition, and for good reason. If the exegetical work on the text is primarily academic, the transmission of that material to the pew is not. Pentecostals may feel unjustly accused of exegeting their experience rather than Scripture, but they will gladly and positively answer the charge of exegeting their congregations. Pentecostals have always been strong on application even if what they were applying has at times been ambiguous!

### The Need for Spiritual Illumination

The final locus of hermeneutics has to be the particular congregation that the preacher faces at any given time. At some point, he or she has to move from hermeneutics of the study to hermeneutics of the pulpit. Reference is made later to this distinction. Here the preacher is more or less ignorant of the real needs of his or her congregation so the real thrust of his or her hermeneutics is vague.

Broadly speaking, three stages of interpretation present themselves: the pure exegetical work;[1] the general implications for

---

[1] Gordon Fee, *Issues in New Testament Hermeneutics*. (Peabody MA: Hendrickson Publishers Inc., 1991), 4, n. 5. I am using Gordon Fee's suggested usage, "*Exegesis* is in fact concerned with what the text meant in its historical context. *Hermeneutics* has to do with the science of interpretation in all its ramifications. . . I will use the term to refer to what the biblical text means for us in terms of our understanding and obedience."

our time and culture, and the specific need of a particular audience. While the academic work must be dependent on the Spirit's anointing, each stage is decreasingly academic in approach, and thus greater illumination, and possibly revelation (in terms of the preaching context) of the Holy Spirit is necessary.

Precisely here Pentecostals have emphasized the anointing of the Holy Spirit, and on this basis emphasize the primary place of prayer in preparation where, "one must seek the anointing on preparation for the sermon."[1] Joseph Kendall Byrd goes on to say:

> The primary focus for anointing in preparation and study is upon prayer. In a work written by eight Assemblies of God preachers, prayer was noted most often as the primary means of sermon preparation. Most of these authors note that prayer is the "source of the anointing." The anointing of the Holy Spirit . . . "is prayed down from heaven." Alice Luce contends that anointing comes from prayer, not study. However, the anointing gives insight and inspires the intellect for preparation. The source of the anointing is strictly prayer.[2]

Byrd continues that prayer may be in "tongues," and such praying, "in the Spirit is communication with God which edifies the preacher."[3] In addition, the pentecostal preacher as a witness to God's revelation "does not go to the text for facts about God. The witness goes to the Bible to encounter a presence and hear God's voice speaking 'ever anew.' The witness testifies about what is seen and heard in the encounter with the presence and voice of God in the biblical text."[4]

---

[1] Joseph Kendall Byrd, *Formulation of a Classical Pentecostal Homiletic in Dialogue with Contemporary Protestant Homiletics*. (Ph.D. dissertation, Southern Baptist Theological Seminary, 1990), 76.
[2] Byrd, *Pentecostal Homiletic*, 76–77.
[3] Byrd, *Pentecostal Homiletic*, 77.
[4] Byrd, *Pentecostal Homiletic*, 210–211.

# Anointed Preaching

In contrast to Byrd's somewhat mechanical description, James Forbes sees a need that, "Those being encouraged to stake their lives on the power and faithfulness of the Spirit would wish for some definite experience to undergird commitment and trust. . . . If that power cannot lift us above despair, it will be difficult to believe in its power to lift us beyond death."[1] He documents too his experience of the intercessory presence of the Holy Spirit in preparation, when "the Spirit helps us in our weakness, for we do not know how to pray as we ought":

> I knelt at my bed, stretched forth my arms and moved my shoulders in writhing jerks of anguish. All I could utter were sighs and groans. But afterwards, I felt so much better that I said, "Perhaps I can pray now." But it seemed the Spirit said to me, "You don't need to pray anymore now. Heaven is equipped to receive choreographed prayer. Also your sighs and groans have already been decoded and help is on the way."[2]

Here is a classic example of what the Pentecostals would call "praying in the Spirit with groans that words cannot express,"[3] and the occurrence reckoned as part of the anointing process during preparation. This is not a contrived experience, if contrived it is inauthentic, but it frequently issues out of a desperation of inadequacy, and is a Spirit-driven search for that spiritual insight needed to communicate the Gospel.

The danger here is that the seeking for illumination as described above will take precedence over and even modify the text to the preacher's agenda, and this error is too frequent. However, it must be emphasized that the illumination required is especially for the application of the text to the occasion of preaching. The application can still be founded on solid exegesis—

---

[1] James Forbes, *The Holy Spirit and Preaching*. (Nashville TN: Abingdon Press, 1989), 72.
[2] Forbes, *The Holy Spirit and Preaching*, 73.
[3] Romans 8:26.

"illumination" that replaces or undermines exegetical work can hardly be considered anointing by the Holy Spirit. After all, the Holy Spirit wrote the book!

Whatever the experiences, the need for prayer is clear. Prayer for any work of God is a motherhood issue, and the apostles recognized that the ministry of the word and prayer especially went together.[1]

**The Need for Spiritual Confirmation**

But Forbes also sees other operations of the Holy Spirit working in preparation. One is what he calls eschatological epistemology—belief in the future as revealed in Scripture—based on the witness of the Spirit of God to our spirit:[2]

> The Spirit's relationship to the future exceeds our comprehension. The Spirit has a way of convincing us that the plan of redemption is working and everything will come out all right and that in every threatening thing and in every comforting thing, the Lord is working to fulfil God's promise about what shall be.[3]

For Forbes, this experience is a continuation of the ongoing experience of the Spirit; "for in the anointing we become aware of a fundamental truth: the Spirit is *in the process* with which we are involved."[4] He characterizes collaboration with the Holy Spirit as a "tag-team relationship" by which "much of the anxiety and dread associated with the preparation process is removed . . ."[5]

---

[1] Acts 6:4.
[2] Romans 8:16.
[3] Forbes, *The Holy Spirit and Preaching*, 75.
[4] Forbes, *The Holy Spirit and Preaching*, 79, where he quotes John 16:12–13; his emphasis.
[5] Forbes, *The Holy Spirit and Preaching*, 80.

## Tedium and the Spirit

The foregoing illustrates the essential knowledge desired and needed through the anointing process of the Holy Spirit. But the danger is that the foregoing can be viewed idealistically and might indicate that following prayer and a sense of anointing the sermon will write itself. Furthermore, the possibility arises that all thoughts following prayer will be attributed to the Holy Spirit with the attendant dangers that flow from a perceived sense of personal infallibility. Here again, Byrd shows a lack of critical perception, and does not address the issue. The little girl exhibited simple common sense, who, watching her father prepare a sermon, asked,

> "How do you know what to say?"
> "God tells me," he answered.
> "Then why do you keep crossing it out?" she asked.[1]

Most will recognize instead the hacking and grinding away that so often appears to be the preacher's lot as he prepares his sermon. To George Sweazey this is part of the Spirit's work in preparation:

> God helps only those who are straining and suffering, but prayer brings understanding that will direct the hard strivings in the right directions. . . . God gives understanding to the preacher through the insights that come to him all through his life; all of his experiences are interpreted from the standpoint of his faith in Christ. Everything that happens to him thus builds up in him a wisdom that is greater than his own. All this slowly acquired understanding is at his disposal as he prepares his sermon.[2]

Forbes agrees. He reviews the Spirit's work in the conception of Jesus, the conception of John in Elizabeth's barren womb, and

---

[1] Quoted by George E. Sweazey, *Preaching the Good News*. (Englewood Cliffs NJ: Prentice-Hall Inc., 1976), 41.
[2] Sweazey, *Preaching the Good News*, 41–42.

recognizes the Spirit "hover[ing] through the process of gestation" until the children were "brought forth," and sees an analogy with the preparation and delivery of the sermon:

> And so it is with sermon development. The Spirit is with us during conception, gestation, and even during the moment of delivery. . . . We even have to learn to endure pain. In fact, the sign of pain is a good one. Those who avoid pain and struggle will not bring forth life in the pulpit. Indeed, the pain is likely to intensify just before a breakthrough can occur.[1]

## Human Resources and Simplicity

All this points to the fact that the Spirit uses human resources, which is remarkable in view of their meagreness, whether knowledge or experience, but also points to the possibility of direct revelation or gifting by the Spirit where necessary. This, in turn, is the basis for two apparently conflicting truths.

First, the use of human resources requires the utmost diligence in exegetical research to provide personal resources for the Spirit's use, not only knowledge but also personal integrity. Spirit anointing is all pervasive upon the whole person and as such, there is no clear demarcation between the work of God's Spirit and human resources. Forbes recognizes this particularly in the "ebb and flow of movement in the power of the Spirit":

> The Spirit carries us so forcefully that the traditional distinctions of preparation of the preacher, preparation of the sermon, preparation for delivery, and the delivery of the sermon itself become subsidiary.[2]

Thus, there is no place for the denial of the need for study originally pursued by earlier Pentecostals. In the 1940s Harold

---

[1] Forbes, *The Holy Spirit and Preaching*, 85–86.
[2] Forbes, *The Holy Spirit and Preaching*, 77.

Horton inveighed against biblical criticism, learning the original languages of the Bible, newer translations, and psychology[1]:

> Human academic knowledge and faith are contrary principles. If we deliberately foster either, the other fades into insignificance. . . . The glory of Pentecost still is that simple men without much learning or culture are producing all over the world spiritual results superior to all the brilliant flower of the academics.[2]

Yet Horton's stand raises the second and apparently paradoxical truth: simple and uneducated men *are* used in proclaiming the Gospel; in fact, that is how Christianity began,[3] and continues in many parts of the undeveloped world. Any hermeneutic must allow for the unlearned, the simple to preach using whatever meagre resources he has.

There is no place for pride. Whatever resources we may have garnered for the proclamation of the Gospel will always be meagre, and in the final analysis the Spirit's use of those resources, not their amount, makes them effective. It is not more anointing for less education, but rather that all education is in itself insufficient. Thus, we all need a sense of our incompetence for the task—that we are among the foolish things of the world that God chose to shame the wise.[4]

## THE EXPERIENCE OF SPIRIT ANOINTING ON DELIVERY

### What It Isn't!

The idea of anointed preaching is known better by its caricature, than for its character; by reputation than from the scriptural record. On this basis, most informed pentecostal preachers can say what it

---

[1] Harold Horton, *Preaching and Homiletics.* (Luton, Beds. UK: Assemblies of God Publishing House, 1946), 12–21.
[2] Harold Horton, *Preaching and Homiletics,* 16–17.
[3] Acts 4:13.
[4] 1 Corinthians 1:27.

is not, even if a clear definition eludes them. Byrd, referring to a number of pentecostal authors writes:

> "Anointing" is not laziness in preparation in which the preacher goes unprepared to speak, expecting the Holy Spirit to fill his/her mouth. Anointing is not "cheap emotional manipulation" working responsive listeners to "a shout." While the anointing is a work of the Holy Spirit, it is not regeneration, sanctification, nor the initial experience of Spirit-baptism. Generally, Pentecostals do not argue that "anointing" infers the Holy Spirit is directly speaking in the sermon. Most Pentecostals believe that the Holy Spirit inspires the individual preacher. The anointing will result in a change of voice and gestures, but boisterous delivery cannot be identified as the anointing.[1]

Most Evangelicals would heartily concur, and James Earl Massey also recognizes that anointed preaching is more than enthusiasm:

> Enthusiasm has meant many things to many people, and the term has been used in connection with both worthy and unworthy experiences. Enthusiasm has been linked with celestial inspiration, poetic fervour, fancied inspiration, ardent feeling, ill-regulated feeling, irrational agitation and movement, ardent zeal, emotionalism, etc., some of these states being too passionate to be rational and too individual to be trusted.[2]

Neither should charisma "be confused with communalism, which is but a sense of contagious engagement between preacher and people."[3] Too often the rapport between congregation and preacher

---

[1] Byrd, *Pentecostal Homiletic*, 70–71.
[2] James Earl Massey, *The Sermon in Perspective*. (Grand Rapids MI: Baker Book House, 1976), 105–106.
[3] Massey, *Sermon in Perspective*, 106.

can be mistaken for the Spirit's unifying and thus condoning presence.

## Lack of Research

J. Daniel Baumann, in his *Introduction to Contemporary Preaching* also has a chapter on the Holy Spirit. He is aware of experiences of the empowering work of the Spirit, but is sceptical of the possibility of documentation. He cites studies done on this issue, but considers that:

> Any study of the Holy Spirit is filled with difficulty, for the subject is not of the laboratory variety. One cannot study this subject in the so-called scientific manner. Empirical research is neither likely nor possible. The Holy Spirit has never been, nor is apt to be, an object for scientific analysis.[1]

He goes on to say, "There is unfortunately a dearth of literature specifically concerned with this subject. Theological treatments of pneumatology are common; treatises, essays or books on the relation of the Holy Spirit to preaching are not."[2] There has been a failure of leadership, first by Pentecostals in an area of great importance to them, but also by Evangelicals who have, albeit ambiguously, recognized this lack. Thus the subject necessarily needs reflection.

Forbes has listed a number of reasons for this apparent lack. They include a risk of appearing unsophisticated in the secular, modern age we live in, and reticence about being identified with problematic stereotypical doctrines. But his main concern is the possibility of loss of control. Thus:

> . . . respectful distance—not only from experiencing the Spirit, but also from language about the Holy Spirit—may

---

[1] J. Daniel Baumann, *An Introduction to Contemporary Preaching.* (Grand Rapids MI: Baker Book House, 1972), 278

[2] Baumann, *Contemporary Preaching*, 278

seem to be the better part of wisdom, especially for moderns who are given to quantification and control. Consequently, the Holy Spirit is less understood, less experienced, and doesn't have a place in the world view or the sacred cosmos of most of us.[1]

## Recorded Experiences

However, in opposition to Baumann's scepticism are many cases of the anointing activity of the Holy Spirit as an experienced truth. This has, of course, been documented by Pentecostals whose philosophy is that the Christian life is to be both learned scripturally and demonstrated experientially. Jesse K. Moon defines the anointing as:

> . . . the special presence of the Holy Spirit in the life and ministry of God's servant which produces an inspiring awareness of the divine presence. His entire faculties are enhanced (heightened illumination, courage, wisdom, discernment, faith, guidance, memory, vocabulary, emotions, intellect, and physical performance) beyond natural abilities. The word of God is quickened to accomplish its regenerating, healing, edifying, and sanctifying objective. And those ministered to are invested with a God-consciousness; a spiritual enlivening; and an interest in, acceptance of, and response to the life and ministry of the anointed.[2]

This type of experiential empowering is also frequently recorded among non-Pentecostal preachers. Charles Haddon Spurgeon was aware of this sense of anointing:

> The divine Spirit will sometimes work upon us so as to bear us completely out of ourselves. From the beginning of

---

[1] Forbes, *The Holy Spirit and Preaching*, 22–23.
[2] Jesse K. Moon, "The Holy Spirit in Preaching," *Paraclete,* 11, (Fall 1977) 26.

the sermon to the end we might at such times say, "Whether in the body or out of the body I cannot tell: God knoweth." . . . I am distinctly conscious of a power working upon me when I am speaking in the name of the Lord, infinitely transcending any personal power of fluency, and far surpassing any energy derived from excitement such as I have felt when delivering a secular lecture or making a speech—so utterly distinct from such power that I am quite certain it is not of the same order or class as the enthusiasm of the politician or the glow of the orator. May we full often feel [sic] the divine energy, and speak with power.[1]

Martyn Lloyd-Jones, in his book *Preachers and Preaching* in a chapter on the Holy Spirit's relationship to preaching, is particularly moved by the experience of the Spirit's anointing:

It gives clarity of thought, clarity of speech, ease of utterance, a great sense of authority and confidence as you are preaching, an awareness of a power not your own thrilling through the whole of your being, and an indescribable sense of joy. You are a man 'possessed,' you are taken hold of, and taken up, . . . It is not your effort; you are just the instrument, the channel, the vehicle: and the Spirit is using you, and you are looking on in great enjoyment and astonishment. There is nothing that is in any way comparable to this. That is what the preacher himself is aware of.[2]

Lloyd-Jones also gives a lengthy review of the scriptural precedents, and then documents widespread historical occurrences of the clear empowering of the Holy Spirit in the history of

---

[1] Charles Haddon Spurgeon, "the Holy Spirit and the Ministry of Preaching," *Theories of Preaching, Selected Readings in the Homiletical Tradition*, ed., Richard Lischer. (Durham NC: The Labrinth Press, 1987), 318.

[2] Lloyd-Jones, *Preaching and Preachers*, 324.

Protestantism. He cites Hugh Latimer, John Livingstone, Cotton Mather, Jonathan Edwards, David Brainerd, Gilbert Tennant, Whitefield and the Wesleys, and many others as having recorded special empowerment of the Holy Spirit during their preaching years.[1]

Massey documents the concept of charismatic or anointed service more clearly. It:

> reflects at least six features which we experience through grace: (1) a sense of assertiveness by which to act; (2) a sense of being identified with divine will; (3) a perceived intensity because what is done relates to the highest frame of reference; (4) a sense of self-transcendence; (5) a kind of instinct for what is done; and (6) a knowledge that the deed is avowedly moral and religious in nature and reason, which is to say that the deed is traceable to God's prompting and power, and that it happens for his own reasons.[2]

## Naiveté and the Holy Spirit

The injunction to become like a child is relevant to this discussion. To be innocent as doves does not mean ignorance; we still need to be as shrewd as snakes![3] For those not gifted with "political savvy," preaching to a congregation with all its hidden agendas is a daunting prospect. The gifts of the Spirit are needed in the pulpit ministry—those most referred to are knowledge and wisdom[4]—to assure the word finds its mark. Even for those able to naturally discern the underlying needs of a congregation, there is still need for innocence.

---

[1] Lloyd-Jones, *Preachers and preaching*, 315–323.
[2] Massey, *Sermons in Perspective*, 102.
[3] Matthew 10:16.
[4] Donald Gee, *Spiritual Gifts in the Work of the Ministry Today.* (Springfield MI: Gospel Publishing House, 1963), 24–27. He reviews pentecostal views on these two gifts, as well as a review of some lexical authorities.

Although speaking from a counselling point of view, Wayne Oates calls for a "disciplined naiveté" which is eminently applicable to preaching:

> Disciplined naiveté is a necessary condition of the effective work of the Holy Spirit in even the most informed mind and memory. The preconceptions, presuppositions, biases, beloved hypotheses, and managed perfections of the legalist, the moralist, or the exhorter are "bracketed in." They are kept in abeyance. This "bracketing in" is a "disconnection" of previous memories, value judgements and decisions *in order* that the pure reality of the moment may be perceived to the fullest.[1]

Oates bases his arguments on Jesus' promise to the disciples to remind them of his sayings, particularly in crisis situations,[2] and he relates Stephen's inspired speech as an example.[3] The parallel with modern preaching as Oates sees it, is in facing the deadly games that people play that "end up in the courtroom, the surgery, or the morgue. . . . They want the pastor to give them *the* answer now." The problem is that the "counsellor could easily give him 'the answer,' but he cannot give him the understanding."[4]

To be able to set aside ones preconceptions, not only in the study but in the pulpit, and to allow the Holy Spirit to inform and guide the sermon is at once the most obvious, yet the most difficult challenge for the preacher. But as with the New Testament disciples, this process provides not only the clear articulation needed, but the most irrefutable logic. Oates' understanding of an evangelistic encounter with an individual has its parallel in preaching:

---

[1] Wayne Oates, *The Holy Spirit in Five Worlds*. (New York NY: Association Press, 1968), 66–67.

[2] Wayne Oates, *The Holy Spirit in Five Worlds*, 60–62, where he quotes Matthew 10:19–20. Mark 13:11, Luke 12:11–12; 21:12–15 and John 14:25–27.

[3] Wayne Oates, *The Holy Spirit in Five Worlds*, 62–63.

[4] Wayne Oates, *The Holy Spirit in Five Worlds*, 64.

We would do better to bracket in our own beliefs and biases and move on the assumption of the Living Presence of the Holy Spirit only. The main discipline is prayer that we might *understand* this person in his totality, to perceive the world from within him as he perceives it. This revelation that comes to us when we permit him to be the self that he is, is a gift of the Spirit. The most carefully worded apology can be easily "withstood and contradicted." A disciplined defencelessness and an inspired understanding of the individual cannot. Whether he likes it or not the "Good News" of God comes to him in such an encounter of openness and teachableness on our part.[1]

### SUMMARY

Clearly, there is much misinformation and misuse of the idea of anointed preaching. This chapter has attempted to establish what is meant by anointed preaching, both the popular view with its attendant problems and projected solutions, and what is an acceptable view.

The documented experiences, giving an overall idea of "preaching beyond ourselves," are viewed through two lenses: the idea that all study and preaching of the word requires illumination by the Holy Spirit, but also that all preaching must remain true to the word that the Spirit wrote in the first place. Much "anointed" preaching holds to the former without the guidance of the latter.

Anointing is not restricted to the act of preaching only, although that may be where it is recognized, but is needed in the preparation of the sermon if the truth is to be recognized by the hearers. The chapter has documented the experience of Spirit

---

[1] Wayne Oates, *The Holy Spirit in Five Worlds*, 68.

## Anointed Preaching

involvement in preparation and many of the factors of preparation that are alleviated by the Spirit's intervention.

Finally, the chapter has dealt with the experience of anointed delivery of the sermon by many past and current preachers, showing its ongoing effect in several areas of the preacher's experience. Massey reminds us that the "sermons we create are always less than the texts we use"[1]—a sharp rebuke to our pride, and that "anointing is to benefit the community,"[2]—not the preacher; a corrective to our motivation.

---

[1] Massey, *The Sermon*, 112.
[2] Massey, *The Sermon*, 108.

Bryan Norford

# 2

## THE THEOLOGICAL BASIS FOR ANOINTED PREACHING

> *For who among men knows the thoughts of a man except the man's spirit within him? In the same way no one knows the thoughts of God except the Spirit of God. We have not received the spirit of the world but the Spirit who is from God, that we may understand what God has freely given us.*
>
> *1 Corinthians. 2:11–12*

Chapter one has laid out some understanding of the nature of anointed preaching, and the recognized and common experience of anointed preaching inside and outside of pentecostal circles. But the experience is pointless, even misleading if it does not find some reference point in Scripture. This chapter seeks to lay this scriptural framework by reviewing the idea of anointing in Scripture in relation to preaching, and by recognizing the illuminating work of the Holy Spirit as part of the anointing process. In doing so, some relevant areas of hermeneutics will be reviewed where these appear at variance with the Spirit's illuminating work and the effect of variances on the accepted philosophy of interpretation.

Pentecostals have been fiercely biblical in their preaching, even if the approach to interpretation can be criticized, as Gordon Fee notes Dunn, Bruner, Hollenweger and Pinnock suggest.[1] Loyalty to the word grew out of a fundamentalist belief in its inspiration: their suggested lack of faithfulness to it was caused by their anti-intellectualism, arising in opposition to the educated "modernists." Even today, this attitude frequently fosters a paradoxical belief in the Bible's clear mandate for life and faith, yet irreverence for the text in preaching. This has been clearly recognized by many, and an attempt to come to grips with the anomaly has provided a spate of literature (by pentecostal standards!) searching for a hermeneutic that would serve the pentecostal community with integrity. While the emerging pentecostal hermeneutic is beyond the scope of this thesis, never-the-less, the illuminating work of the Spirit is relevant both to a pentecostal hermeneutic and to the anointing work of the Spirit. As chapter one characterized anointed preaching as "preaching beyond ourselves," there is a corollary of anointed preparation we may characterize as "knowing beyond ourselves":

> . . . no one knows the thoughts of God except the Spirit of God. We have not received the spirit of the world but the Spirit who is from God, that we may understand what God has freely given us.[2]

## THE RELATIONSHIP OF HERMENEUTICS TO PREACHING

### Hermeneutics in the Pulpit

The previous chapter referred to the "hermeneutics of the study." This chapter considers "hermeneutics of the pulpit." The work of

---

[1] Gordon Fee and Douglas Stuart. *Gospel and Spirit: Issues in New Testament Hermeneutics.* (Peabody MA: Hendrickson, 1991), 83–84.

[2] 1 Corinthians 2:11–12.

hermeneutics must eventually move from pure exegetical work—understanding what the text meant to its authors—into the significance for us today. While the original meaning may be static—as far as research and our understanding allow—the significance is related to the time, place and circumstances of the interpretive procedure. I suggest that the double authorship of Scripture, human and divine, relates to this phenomenon. But the problem arising is the possibility of double meaning clearly expressed by Gordon Fee:

> If indeed God intends something beyond what the human author intended—and I would certainly not deny that possibility—then who speaks for God? That is, who determines the deeper meaning God intends for us? The Magisterium? The Dispensationalist's view of history? I admit to being squeamish regarding the whole area.[1]

Yet, once the author's original intended meaning has been established, the significance of that meaning for an audience is time and place specific. Thus, a treatise on a particular passage may well have general significance for a culture for a period of time, but a Sunday sermon on the same passage of Scripture, might be quite different within the parameter of meaning and not at all significant to any other congregation.

Thus, the illuminating work of the Spirit in hermeneutics is essential. The preacher particularly is aware of the need for illumination of the text for a particular audience. This need arises because of the lack of certainty of the needs of the audience, the lack being greater the less the preacher knows the audience. The hermeneutics of the study must eventually become the hermeneutics of the pulpit; the development of the general meaning of the text must eventually develop into the text's significance for the immediate congregation. If we need the enlightening of the Holy Spirit to aid our academic pursuit of the

---

[1] Gordon Fee, *Gospel and Spirit*, 19.

text's original meaning, that assistance must also be necessary to direct our sense to the need of a specific congregation. Many preachers have given voice to the fact that it is rarely possible to preach the same sermon twice without reworking. The significance of the passage for another audience at another time has changed.

The concern of this book is for the hermeneutics of the pulpit, remembering the illuminating Spirit is the one who also anoints. Thus, the philosophy of pentecostal hermeneutics that is prior to preaching, which we have designated as "knowing beyond ourselves" requires review.

## Expansion of the Preacher's Resources

The concept of a pneumatic epistemology introduced later in the chapter, or the more common idea of the extra sense of knowing from the Holy Spirit, is frequent throughout the literature that recognizes the anointing work of the Holy Spirit in preaching. This will be seen in a number of later references, but typical is Guy Duffield in *Pentecostal Preaching*: that it is "particularly characteristic of a Spirit-anointed ministry, wherein the man of God preaches better than he knows."[1] Donald Gee includes the use of the gifts of the Spirit in the ministry of the word—particularly the word of wisdom and the word of knowledge.[2] Byrd, adds, "The anointing causes the preacher to preach with authority and causes the Spirit-filled listeners to recognize it, not as the preacher's authority, but as the authority of the Holy Spirit."[3] Several scriptural examples come to mind: the witness of the Spirit within, typified by the burning hearts of the two on the road to Emmaus,[4]

---

[1] Guy P. Duffield Jr., *Pentecostal Preaching*. (New York: Vantage Press, c. 1956), 33.
[2] Donald Gee, *Spiritual Gifts*, 29.
[3] Byrd, *Pentecostal Homiletic*, 78.
[4] Luke 24:32.

Jeremiah's "fire in the bones";[1] the command not to think ahead in situations of opposition[2] and Stephen's unanswerable logic.[3]

This sense of our natural incapacity to preach is at the heart of the widespread experience of preaching beyond ourselves among many preachers, and is the core of anointed preaching. Acknowledgement of this inadequacy is fertile ground for the Holy Spirit's work in anointing. But inadequacy is not ignorance—ignorance is fertile ground only for variance from Scripture, and here the danger is falling prey to the two extremes; either rejoicing in ignorance that may provide opportunity for the Spirit, or smugness and pride in the sense of control that knowledge brings. The Holy Spirit will expand the resources we place at his disposal, but not replace wilful ignorance.

Thus, as we shall see, sloth claims that the gathering of knowledge and personal skill is not required. Quite the reverse; they are a necessity. Paradoxically, for the humble, the greater the gathering of knowledge the greater the sense of ignorance. Probably one of the greatest obstacles to true anointed preaching is the sense of control gained from "sufficient" knowledge. But it is illusory and in the end self-defeating for the aspiring preacher of the Gospel.

## THE SCRIPTURAL PATTERN OF SPIRIT ANOINTING

The scriptural significance of the anointing goes back to the Old Testament, and appendix one gives an overview of the roots of the idea for its use in the New. Both Old and New Testaments occasionally use both anointing and the coming of the Spirit on individuals at one time, suggesting two ideas are either interchangeable or closely related. Thus it is likely the anointing is far more significant than the occurrence of the word would imply.

---

[1] Jeremiah 20:9.
[2] Matthew 10:19–20.
[3] Acts 6:9–10.

Roger Stronstad points out, for instance, that the charismatic activities recorded in the Old Testament were typically programmatic, only giving examples of ongoing phenomena:

> Evidently, none of the biblical narrators ever felt that it was necessary to make explicit every example of charismatic activity. They appear to have been content to give programmatic descriptions of a charismatic ministry which was far greater than a statistical count of these narratives would imply.[1]

Illustrating this, the absence of surprise at the prophesying of the seventy elders suggests it was not an uncommon occurrence, yet the unorthodox prophesying of Eldad and Medad within the camp aroused consternation.[2]

## Permanence of the Anointing

The Old Testament idea of enablement was for an ongoing "anointing." Saul, David and Elisha, for example, all received an anointing at the beginning of service, until their service was terminated by God's removal of his Spirit or by death. This is consistent with the idea of the resident Spirit within the believer, and also consistent with the traditional pentecostal doctrine of the initial baptism of the Holy Spirit of the believer. Similarly, appendix one indicates a wider application of the idea of anointing than the few occurrences of the word for anointing initially suggests in the New Testament.

Furthermore, Jesus' own understanding of his anointing for the task of preaching was an ongoing enablement.[3] This has been further argued by Gary M. Burge as he points out that the Gospel writers in the record of Jesus' water baptism tended to "shift their emphasis away from the baptism to the anointing of Jesus by the

---

[1] Roger Stronstad, *The Charismatic Theology of St. Luke*. (Peabody MA: Hendrickson Publishers, 1984), 17.
[2] Numbers 11:24–27
[3] Cf. Luke 4:18 with Matthew 11:5; Luke 7:22

Spirit."[1] In particular, he reminds us that John recognized Jesus, "not through water baptism, but in the Spirit's descent."[2] He also refers to John's use of *menein*: the Spirit *remained* upon him.[3]

In relation to preaching, the idea of a permanent anointing also has its parallel the personal "call" into ministry, confirmed by ordination of the one called This is true for the pentecostal movement, as well as others.[4] Lloyd-Jones documents this idea of anointing for service as an experience of call. Speaking of the sense of constraint, he writes:

> I would say that only the man who is called to preach is the man who cannot do anything else, in the sense that he is not satisfied with anything else. This call to preach is so put upon him, and such pressure comes to bear upon him that he says, "I can do nothing else. I must preach."[5]

This parallels Jeremiah's experience, who despite his unpopularity and persecution, was driven to admit:

> But if I say, "I will not mention him or speak any more in his name," his word is in my heart like a fire, a fire shut up in my bones. I am weary of holding it in; indeed I cannot.[6]

And possibly Paul's experience:

> Yet when I preach the gospel, I cannot boast, for I am compelled to preach. Woe to me if I do not preach the gospel![7]

---

[1] Gary M. Burge, *The Anointed Community, The Holy Spirit in the Gospel of John*. (Grand Rapids MI: Eerdmans Publishing Co., 1987), 51.
[2] Burge, *The Anointed Community*, 52
[3] Burge, *The Anointed Community*, 54
[4] The Certificate of Ordination of the Pentecostal Assemblies of Canada emphasizes the phrase "PREACH THE WORD" among all other facets of Christian ministry, by using capitals and centering the phrase on its own line.
[5] Lloyd-Jones, *Preaching and Preachers*, 105.
[6] Jeremiah 20:9.
[7] 1 Corinthians 9:16.

## The Intermittent Character of the Anointing

But despite the idea of an ongoing anointing, both the Old and New Testaments convey the idea that the anointing can also be augmented on occasion as the need arises. This idea, the permanent *and* intermittent nature of the anointing, is not universally accepted by Pentecostals. Byrd maintains that the traditional pentecostal understanding of operating "under the anointing" is a "special anointing of the Holy Spirit for a particular occasion, that can be given to any Spirit-filled individual." In this case, he does not appear to consider original baptism in the Holy Spirit to be an ongoing anointing.[1] Further:

> It is basically defined as power for special occasions. . . . It is the *anticipated* characteristic of the called Spirit-filled preacher. Anointing occurs in two stages: in study and preparation; and in the delivery of the sermon.[2]

Byrd does not attempt to give a scriptural basis for this two stage anointing process in preparation and delivery, which he can only derive from experience. In addition, Byrd's record does not support his claim. In quoting pentecostal sources he appears to agree with anointing as an ongoing function. He writes:

> David Bundrick, a pentecostal educator, defines Spirit-anointing as those occasions when an individual is "appointed to fulfil a special function," the Holy Spirit comes upon this individual to "confer power and enablement" for the task. The concept of Spirit-anointing is drawn from the biblical image of anointing of kings and prophets in the Old Testament. The New Testament concept of anointing is viewed as a fulfilment of the Old Testament image in the charismatic enduement of power.[3]

---

[1] Byrd, "*Pentecostal Homiletic*," 44–45.
[2] Byrd, "*Pentecostal Homiletic*, 122, my emphasis.
[3] Byrd, "*Pentecostal Homiletic*, 45

Byrd's failure on this point is symptomatic of his attempt to formulate his homiletic to accommodate pentecostal tradition and belief without calling contradictions into question; to reflect on rather than react with pentecostal material, even from a pentecostal viewpoint. The same failure will be apparent later in the evidences of Spirit anointing and absence of the mention of the fruit of the Spirit.

However, the idea of an on-going and intermittent anointing is consistent in the Old Testament as appendix one sets out. The New Testament sees the same idea in the pentecostal claim of the initial filling or baptism on the day of Pentecost and also the later filling by the Spirit of the same individuals on critical occasions.[1] Byrd recognizes this, and refers to it as the "dual nature of Spirit-baptism."[2] He quotes Stronstad who, in describing terminology, suggests that:

> . . . a twofold distinction must be made. The terms "anointed" and "baptized" describe the consecrating work of the Holy Spirit in inaugurating one's public ministry. The terms "filled," "clothed," and "empowered" describe the actual equipping by the Spirit for that ministry. Here, then, is the distinction between the once-for-all and the repetitive character of the gift of the Spirit. The consecration by the Spirit is once-for-all, while, as the need arises, the equipping by the Spirit is repetitive.[3]

However, despite the necessary penchant for clear definitions, even these definitions are not clear. Stronstad's own research has indicated the great variety of terminology used in the Spirit's charismatic activity in the Old Testament.[4] In the New Testament, the terms baptism and filling are used interchangeably. For

---

[1] Note also the present imperative to be "filled with the Spirit," Ephesians 5:18, and the "special" filling of the disciples at critical times in Acts 4:8, 31; 7:55.
[2] Byrd, *Pentecostal Homiletic*, 40.
[3] Stronstad, *Charismatic Theology*, 81.
[4] Stronstad, *Charismatic Theology*, 18.

example, the "filling" on the day of Pentecost was also understood as the "baptism" by the apostles.[1] However, the two-fold distinction is clear, even if the definitions are not. The review in appendix one indicates anointing clearly refers to ongoing enablement for a designated function. The repeated empowerment at critical times is part of the ongoing enablement of the Spirit.

**The Relationship to Spirit Baptism**
We have noted Byrd's ambivalence between anointing and the Pentecostal understanding of the baptism in the Holy Spirit. He maintains that the latter is a prerequisite for the former, although his lack of references to authors suggests that many leading Pentecostals would not be dogmatic about it. It seems clear there is little distinction made between the baptism of the Holy Spirit and the initial "anointing" for service; their synonymy is assumed.[2]

Ray Hughes does not mention the baptism in the Holy Spirit in relation to preaching in his book *Pentecostal Preaching*,[3] while Duffield's book of the same name simply indicates that those who claim Spirit baptism should at least show a "vast difference in the preaching."[4]

Added to this is the general recognition that, "most Pentecostals do not claim that those Christians lacking the experience of Spirit-baptism are not true believers. One may be a true believer without Spirit-baptism."[5] If therefore those without this experience have the Spirit indwelling them, it follows that anointing is possible for all those that God calls, irrespective of experience.[6] Unfortunately, Byrd's position that only the Spirit-

---

[1] Jesus' promise of the baptism of the Holy Spirit predicted by John the Baptist, John 1:33, eventually became the filling of Acts 2:4. Peter also refers to that event as baptism, cf. Acts 1:4–5 and 11:15–16.
[2] Typical is Gary Burge who identifies the two, *Anointed Community*, 52.
[3] Ray H. Hughes, *Pentecostal Preaching*. (Cleveland TN: Pathway Press, 1981).
[4] Guy Duffield, *Pentecostal Preaching*, 23–24.
[5] Byrd, *Pentecostal Homiletic*, 36.
[6] Most Pentecostals cite Romans 8:9 as evidence of a distinction between the indwelling Spirit in all Christians, and the "clothing" in power at Spirit baptism as a

baptised can be anointed for preaching may be what most Pentecostals believe, but the flip side of this assumes no effective preaching after the New Testament Church until the reintroduction of Spirit baptism! This is too close to the claims of the cults to be comfortable.

## PENTECOSTAL TRENDS IN HERMENEUTICS

No examination of anointed preaching can pass without some review of the hermeneutics that drive it. While general hermeneutics are beyond our scope, the hermeneutics that arise in the preparation of anointed preaching are a valid concern, as is the application of Scripture to Christian life generally.[1]

### Current Trends

The positions of current exponents of pentecostal hermeneutics are ably reviewed by Stronstad.[2] The most common is the maintenance of descriptive/historical passages to establish theology, at variance with the prevailing idea that didactive passages take precedence.[3] In general terms this has resulted in prioritising Paul's theology over Luke's, allowing Paul's theology to interpret Luke's.

Stronstad challenges the prevailing "didactive only as normative" methodology on the grounds that the general distinction between didactic and descriptive passages is alien to the New Testament understanding of Old Testament historiography, and in particular, Luke's theological stance within his genre is independent of and not to be interpreted by Paul.[4]

---

second event.

[1] Note Fee's agreement in *Gospel and Spirit* with a student that "the ministry *is* hermeneutics," 24, or better that "Christian life is hermeneutics," 51.

[2] Roger Stronstad, "Trends in Pentecostal Hermeneutics," *Paraclete* 22:3 (Summer 1988), 3-5.

[3] John R. W. Stott, *Baptism and Fullness, The Work of the Holy Spirit Today*, 2nd ed. (London: Intervarsity Press, 1975), 15.

[4] Stronstad, *Charismatic Theology*, 6–12.

Further to the issue of experience is Stronstad's claim that experience forms part of one's presuppositions in hermeneutics. Initially it is not Stronstad's claim, but the claim of others, that the Pentecostal tends to exegete his experience. However, Stronstad claims that the criticism cuts both ways to the benefit of the Pentecostal:

> When Leon Morris admits that the charismata died out in the Early Church he is, as surely as every pentecostal is accused of doing, exegeting his own experience and the experience of earlier generations of non-pentecostals. And if one is to exegete his experience, there can be no question about which experience—pentecostal or non-pentecostal—is the better experience to exegete, for it is the unanimous witness of the Gospels, the Acts, and the Pauline epistles that Jesus, the apostles, and the Early Church generally were all charismatic in their ministry.[1]

William W. Menzies has produced what Stronstad calls a "holistic" hermeneutic, listing inductive, deductive, and (most relevant) verification levels of listening to the text.[2] His inductive level includes a *descriptive* section, arguing for the use of descriptive passages for determining theology, as most of the Bible is written in some descriptive genre.[3]

Gordon Fee has broadened the whole issue of genre and its effect on the interpretation of Scripture for teaching normative Christian behaviour, questioning the restrictive use of the didactic mesh and seeking a theological stance based on the intent of the authors within their selected genre.[4] However, he is more cautious than his contemporaries in establishing normative (mandatory) requirements for spiritual experience, preferring to establish a

---

[1] Roger Stronstad, "Pentecostal Experience and Hermeneutics," *Paraclete* 26:1 (Winter 1992), 16.
[2] Stronstad, "Pentecostal Experience," 5–15.
[3] Stronstad, "Pentecostal Experience," 6.
[4] Gordon Fee, *Gospel and Spirit*, 89-96.

normal (expected) pattern and avoiding "language that seems more obligatory . . . than . . . the New Testament documents themselves."[1]

However, it is important to note that none of the above writers have suggested a change to the universally accepted "one meaning" approach to interpretation of Scripture; nor does this book nor the following suggested hermeneutic by Howard Ervin.

## The Epistemological approach

Of relevance to anointed preaching is Howard Ervin's approach from the epistemological viewpoint.[2] He suggests that when inspired Scriptures are involved the two recognized ways of knowing, namely reason and sensory experience are insufficient. To them there must be added a *pneumatic* epistemology based on the essential illumination of the Holy Spirit within, but also in continuity with the apostolic existential witness of the past.[3]

Here, it seems to me, Ervin is the most pentecostal of the present approaches to pentecostal hermeneutics, in that he recognizes that pentecostal theology must start from first principles, and calls into question the exclusively rational categories traditionally used for hermeneutics. If, as stated earlier, anointed preaching is more than delivery, it is also certainly more than intellect and sensory input, and a hermeneutic based solely on these must be deficient to classify as anointed. Thus Ervin rejects the notion of Bultmann that, "The interpretation of the biblical Scriptures is not subject to any different conditions of understanding from any other literature."[4]

This is the basic reason for the New Hermeneutic calling "myth" what the believer would call "mystery."[5] The strength of

---

[1] Gordon Fee, *Gospel and Spirit*, 102–103
[2] Howard M. Ervin, "Hermeneutics: A Pentecostal Option," *Essays on Apostolic Themes*, ed., Paul Elbert. (Peabody MA: Hendrickson Publishers, Inc. 1985), 23.
[3] Howard M. Ervin, "Hermeneutics: A Pentecostal Option," 33–35.
[4] Howard M. Ervin, "Hermeneutics: A Pentecostal Option," 26.
[5] Howard M. Ervin, "Hermeneutics: A Pentecostal Option," 30.

Ervin's approach is that it attempts to get behind the totally rational approach and inform or modify it with spiritual categories. It is unfortunate that in the debate over pentecostal hermeneutics, this approach has not been given the attention it deserves. Perhaps this approach is too far removed from the burning question of whether "narrative is normative," particularly within the Acts debate, or because the importance of epistemology upon hermeneutics appears to have been overlooked, even rejected. Stronstad writes:

> Though his essay is entitled, "Hermeneutics: A Pentecostal Option," Ervin contributes little to the subject of pentecostal hermeneutics. Apart from a few paragraphs at the end of his essay, he writes primarily about epistemology and not about hermeneutics.[1]

**The Scriptural Approach**

It appears to me that Ervin has suggested a firmer starting point for pentecostal theology in introducing what he calls a *pneumatic* hermeneutic. Although Stronstad has incorporated this factor into his developing hermeneutic,[2] the positions of writers generally apart from Ervin, have been mediated totally from the rationalist viewpoint. Perhaps because the tradition of the protestant hermeneutic is firmly entrenched in the hermeneutical sub-conscious, the formulation is attempted from a variation of the accepted hermeneutical norms using basic rationalist arguments. Surely, a thoroughgoing pentecostal hermeneutic must commence with a pneumatic approach along the lines that Ervin has suggested.

How do we establish a pneumatic hermeneutic interpretation of Scripture? This surely is the prior question when dealing with the establishment of theology from historical or other genres. Is the Spirit's work a mystery beyond our understanding, too subjective

---

[1] Stronstad, "Trends," 9.
[2] Stronstad, "Trends," 26.

to be dependable or too unpredictable to be sufficiently codified for use? If we want to maintain integrity with both Scripture and the Holy Spirit's work, where else can we turn but to the pages of Scripture for established patterns of the Holy Spirit's hermeneutical work? If, as Menzies maintains, the use of historical precedent is warranted in Scripture itself,[1] surely here is a more viable and concrete starting point.

## Informing the Rational Approach

Fee touches on this in his essay on historical precedent. "Whether we can reproduce the manner of exegesis which the New Testament authors applied to the Old Testament may be a moot point." At this point he closes the discussion with an argument from Longenecker that because of the revelatory nature of the New Testament its exegesis should be considered "once-for-all," not normative, and in some cases not even repeatable.[2]

There is some truth to that statement. After all, the New Testament writers, beginning with Jesus himself, were re-evaluating the Old Testament in the light of Christology. That level of re-interpretation is in fact new revelation, and as such is not open to us today; evangelicals hold that, while being progressive, revelation was completed in Jesus Christ.[3] Further, Longenecker shows that within the parameters of their contemporary hermeneutics, the New Testament writer's use of the Old was rationally valid without being "mechanical":

> . . . we must abandon the mistaken idea that the New Testament writer's treatment of the Old Testament was either (1) an essentially mechanical process, whereby explicit "proof-texts" and exact "fulfilments" were brought together, or (2) an illegitimate twisting and distortion of the ancient text. . . . What they were conscious of,

---

[1] Menzies, "Methodology," 10.
[2] Fee, *Gospel and Spirit*, 95, n. 23.
[3] Generally based on Jesus as the final revelation, Hebrews 1:1–2

however, is interpreting the Old Testament (1) from a Christocentric perspective, (2) in conformity with a Christian tradition, and (3) along Christological lines.[1]

If the hermeneutic was not mechanical, it was certainly creative, even illuminated—in this case we should say inspired. However, given the Christological bent of New Testament hermeneutics and the patterns set by the New Testament writers, Longenecker's statement is far too restrictive; the patterns *are* repeatable.

Bernard Ramm describes the Old and New Testaments as parallel rivers, with channels cut between by the New Testament types. He maintains that similar channels can also be cut through which are not specifically named in Scripture. Longenecker's view is closer to the restrictive hermeneutic of Bishop Marsh that only types specifically designated in Scripture are permissible.[2] Either way, interpretive Scripture references like Matthew's typology of Israel with Christ,[3] and Paul's "allegory,"[4] (more likely simply spiritualizing historical facts—a not uncommon pentecostal practice), need greater consideration for inclusion into hermeneutical practice. And what about Paul's "pearl-stringing"[5] and even the occasional proof text?[6]

It should be noted that Evangelicals have in fact adopted some New Testament usage of the Old. The New Testament use of Psalms as prophetic,[7] Acts 2:25–32, 13:35–37, together with other New Testament writers, has given rise to the whole concept of Messianic Psalms; and who has not used Isaiah 53 to refer to Christ?

---

[1] Richard Longenecker, "Can We Reproduce the Exegesis of the New Testament?" *Tyndale Bulletin* 21 (1970)," 6
[2] Bernard Ramm, *Protestant Biblical Interpretation*. (Grand Rapids MI: Baker Book House, 1970), 219–220.
[3] Cf. Matthew 2:15 with Hosea 11:1
[4] Galatians 4:21–31.
[5] Romans 3:10-18, 15:10–12, Galatians 3:10–13 and others.
[6] Galatians 3:16
[7] Cf. Peter's and Paul's use of Psalm 16:8–11 in Acts 2:25–32 and 13:35–37.

The purpose of this book is not to determine appropriate pentecostal hermeneutics, but at least to indicate where the present discussion bears on anointed preaching. It is interesting to note that Ervin's proposal coincides with the issues set out in Longenecker's analysis—not solely mechanical, and in conformance with Christian tradition. The other issues Longenecker lists, Christ-centred interpretation and adherence to Scripture are both established traditions of Pentecostals, even if often violated.

Thus the total rejection of further areas of interpretation by Longenecker seems somewhat incongruous to his findings, and sounds very much like a special hermeneutic of the Holy Spirit, not to be codified. It compares with Rothe's attitude to the New Testament Greek before the discovery of Koiné Greek, that it was a special language of the Holy Ghost.[1]

However, this approach to hermeneutics is not new, although at this point apparently unresolved. According to Longenecker, there are presently three schools of thought maintaining a positive stance to this approach. Conservative interpreters:

> ... hold—or at least 'feel'—that on so vital a matter as the New Testament's use of the Old, the descriptive is also normative; ... but many ... insist that the exegetical methods of Christ and the apostles must control exegetical practices today.[2]

Others also supporting this scriptural approach to interpretation, are existential exegetes who insist that it is "open to us to go beyond the New Testament types and to mention other similar correspondences."[3] For instance, Roman Catholic scholars have developed their doctrine of *sensus plenior* guided by the Magisterium of the Church. Longenecker concludes that while Evangelicals are generally unhappy with the latter two positions,

---

[1] F. F. Bruce, *The books and the Parchments*. (Old Tappan NJ: Fleming H. Revell Co., 3rd edition 1963), 63.
[2] Longenecker, "Can We Reproduce?" 34.
[3] Longenecker, "Can We Reproduce?" 34, Quoting Walther Eichrodt.

they have held to some form of the thesis that the descriptive is also in some manner normative for exegesis today.[1]

If we disallow the methods of the New Testament writers in our interpretation, we are by implication saying that the New Testament writers were taking liberties with the text, or worse still, accusing the Holy Spirit of the same thing. If we believe that God's word can stand up to scrutiny, surely his treatment of Scripture within that word can do the same; it should not have to hide behind his sovereignty.

## Need for a Pneumatic Hermeneutic

While the above may demonstrate the difficulties of arriving at an accepted hermeneutic for general interpretation, it deeply underscores the greater need for flexibility in interpretation for the pulpit, where the Holy Spirit will use Scripture to address specific needs. To recognize the work of the Spirit in this "hermeneutics of the pulpit," is to call for a "pneumatic hermeneutic."

This should not open up a Pandora's box of subjectivism or emotionalism. As Stronstad has pointed out, in relation to the charismatic experience and resulting theological presuppositions this is not true. While they certainly do not guarantee sound interpretation, they:

> . . . do not stand in independence from either cognitive presuppositions or historico-grammatico principles. Rather, experiential presuppositions are but one, albeit important and complementary, element of hermeneutics.[2]

The same is true of hermeneutics based on the pattern of the New Testament. The objective reality of the Bible for the testing of hermeneutical ploys remains, as does the community of faith with its prescribed role of assessment[3] based on the analogy of

---

[1] Longenecker, "Can We Reproduce?" 35.
[2] Stronstad, "Pentecostal Experience," 25.
[3] 1 Corinthians 14:29. While in context this reference deals with the gift of prophecy, it is also particularly relevant to anointed preaching which claims its Spirit-

faith. After all, these are parameters that govern Christian teaching and practice; why should interpretive rules be different? In fact, it could be argued that much aberrant charismatic behaviour might have been better controlled if hermeneutics had that sort of flexibility.

In reviewing present exegesis in the New Testament, Longenecker disallows the revelatory character of *pesher* as being inappropriate for us. Fair enough. But he also allows the *midrash* as appropriate only in so far as it follows the course of modern historical-grammatical exegesis. Accordingly, our present mechanical hermeneutical system is the mesh through which all, including New Testament exegesis, is to be viewed.[1] Longenecker argues "Our commitment as Christians is to the reproduction of the apostolic faith and doctrine, and not necessarily to the specific apostolic exegetical practices."[2] But how can we be sure of the apostolic doctrine if we believe their hermeneutical practices are uncertain?

## SUMMARY

This chapter has attempted to relate the experience of anointed preaching to Scripture, in particular the illuminating work of the Holy Spirit, and to view related hermeneutics from the viewpoint of anointed preaching understood in chapter one. This has given rise to a parallel idea of "preaching beyond ourselves" to "knowing beyond ourselves."

The history of interpretation indicates that while the rational response to runaway fanciful interpretation is essential, the rational approach alone is too restrictive to be adequate. The approach tends to use the same process to rationalize away the Spirit's

---

inspired component.
[1] Longenecker, "Can We Reproduce?" 38.
[2] Richard Longenecker, *Biblical Exegesis in the Apostolic Period.* (Grand Rapids MI: Eerdmans Publishing Co., 1975), 219.

charismatic work as liberal theology does to explain away the inspirational and miraculous work of the Holy Spirit. The charismatic work of the Spirit—in Bultmann terminology—is really a "myth" to the non-Pentecostal.

We maintain the idea that anointed preaching includes the idea of the permanent anointing for the ministry of preaching, synonymous with the "call" to ministry, as well as the intermittent sense of anointing on preaching. It is parallel to the pentecostal idea of the initial filling of an individual by the Spirit, and the intermittent filling at times of crisis or need.

This approach is especially applicable to preaching where application is more clearly identified with a particular audience, than to general studies that have a wider audience and thus less obvious parallels.

The chapter describes the necessity of illumination for a given preaching context, as complementary to the illumination given for exegesis. This gives rise to the idea of pneumatic epistemology—input into knowing by the Holy Spirit in addition to reason and sensory perception. The effect on purely rational interpretation is described for which a modified approach is called for.

# 3

## THE NEED FOR INTEGRITY AND FLEXIBILITY

> *Do your best to present yourself to God as one approved, a workman who does not need to be ashamed and who correctly handles the word of truth.*
> 
> *1 Timothy. 2:15*

The classic distinction between message and method in evangelism, has traditionally been ignored in relation to preaching. This lack is allied to the rational categories used to dictate hermeneutics. In a similar way, sermon formats are based on cognitive content and Greek oratorical categories. These presuppositions have created a rigid format of prescribed sermon types considered as necessary vehicles for the Gospel. This has, and continues to influence pentecostal teaching on homiletics, to the detriment of establishing a genuine anointed preaching.

The content of anointed preaching is the Gospel in its unchanging message and characteristics, but the logical direction for anointed preaching, that has as its base a pneumatic epistemology, must be flexibility. As the methods of promoting evangelism are as flexible as the gifts of the evangelist and the needs and culture of the evangelized dictate, so the ways in which the sermonic vehicle is constructed may vary. This chapter deals not only with the integrity of the message of the Gospel, but also with the flexibility that must be accorded the Holy Spirit in the propagation of that Gospel.

## THE CONTENT AND PURPOSE OF ANOINTED PREACHING

### Problems in Pentecostal Content

By far the greatest import for sermon preparation is content of the sermon. It is here that pentecostal preaching has been widely and justly criticized for poor scriptural content, frequently attributed to the Holy Spirit who "provided" the message. Duffield states a number of problems:

> I have listened to many full gospel preachers without having cause to open my Bible during the entire message. . . . We have been training our people to depend entirely too much on their emotions for their spiritual blessings and stability. Our people are the product of our preaching.[1]

He goes on:

> Have we not often laid more emphasis on the signs than on the preaching of the word? Have we not often rejoiced when the word was not preached and the signs alone were manifested?[2]

Furthermore:

> There is a certain type of preaching that is more or less just about the word of God. It does not give enough specific Scripture on which a person's faith may rest. . . . Our people need to know a great deal more about their Bible. The dearth of actual Bible knowledge among pentecostal people is appalling. It is important that our people be

---

[1] Duffield, *Pentecostal Preaching*, 39.
[2] Duffield, *Pentecostal Preaching*, 47.

informed concerning the word, but it is more important that they have their faith increased through the word.[1]

He adds:

> ... some have mistaken a Holy Ghost preacher for the one who, without any previous thought or preparation, simply gets up and says everything that comes to his mind. You have heard a man take a text and ramble, and never refer to what the text said. When he has finished you have no idea what he actually said. Yet because he made no preparation he thought he was depending on the Lord—and it was called "Pentecostal Preaching."[2]

Experience has shown that a lost appetite for the word is difficult to replace, and providing meaningful content for many pentecostals may be an uphill task. Experience has shown that learning, understanding and absorbing the word competes poorly with "instant spirituality" directly from the Spirit!

## The Relationship of Spirit and Word

Scripture clearly teaches that the Spirit is essential to understanding of the word[3]:

> There cannot be a ministry of the word of God apart from the ministry of the Spirit of God. Jesus did not begin his preaching ministry in Galilee until he was endowed with the Spirit at the Jordan river. There was no preaching until Pentecost on the part of the followers of Jesus, except on the experimental mission where they were deployed as recorded in Matthew chapter ten.[4]

---

[1] Duffield, *Pentecostal Preaching*, 46.
[2] Duffield, *Pentecostal Preaching*, 59–60.
[3] 1 Corinthians 2:11–13.
[4] D. W. Cleverley Ford, *The Ministry of the Word.* (Grand Rapids MI: Eerdmans, 1979), 91.

Thus few would dispute that the word without the Spirit is dead, but many pentecostal preachers give the impression that the word is less important than the Spirit's presence. In fact, the word is essential for the Spirit's transmission of the Gospel. Pierre Marcel, in recognizing that the power of the preached word is by the Spirit, also sees the Spirit's attachment to the word:

> The power of the Gospel and of preaching is bestowed by the Spirit considered as a divine person. According to us Protestants, the Spirit joins himself to and acts *with* the word. The preaching of the word and the action of the Holy Spirit go hand in hand, and as a general rule *the Spirit does not act apart from the word.*[1]

In comparing the Lutheran and Reformed theology of the relation of the word to the Spirit's mission, Hendrikus Berkhof recognizes weaknesses in both positions, but his analysis of the Reformed position is relevant:

> They preferred to describe the working of the Spirit as occurring "together with the word," *cum verbo*. They did not dare to say that that where the word is the Spirit is also. The Spirit can work outside of the word and the preached word can remain without effect. . . . The dangerous consequences of this position were bound to come, however. If the opening of the heart does not come through the word itself, but must be expected from another action of the Spirit alongside the word, the hearers are inclined to give little heed to the Word and to wait for the inner signs of the opening of the heart.[2]

According to Berkhof, this inaugurated the Reformed Pietism of the sixteenth and seventeenth centuries, but his characterization

---

[1] Pierre Marcel, *The Relevance of Preaching*, Tr. by Rob Roy McGregor. (Grand Rapids MI: Baker Book House, 1963), 30, his emphasis.

[2] Hendrikus Berkhof, *The Doctrine of the Holy Spirit*. (London: The Epworth Press, undated), 37–38.

has its modern equivalents in the pentecostal movements. Many reformists have become "inclined to give little heed to the word," preferring rather to "wait for the inner signs," resulting in a "basic introversion," and "lack of certainty of faith,"[1] Yet, this is closer to the Arminian roots of Pentecostalism, strands of which are evident in the later Lutheran understanding of the relation of word to Spirit.

> Nevertheless, the word in many cases does not create faith. How can that be explained? Later generations of Lutherans ascribed that lack of result to a certain degree of free will in man, by which he can resist the Spirit.[2]

If it is the free will in man which rejects the word, Pentecostals must be sure it is the word that is being rejected. Experience suggests that it is lack of the word that is being ignored. And if it is lack of the word, here is reason for loss of spiritual power in pentecostal preaching.

## The Purpose is Mission

Berkof has identified the Church's use of spiritual gifts for the up-building of herself—that is, for individual or community comfort or gain—without a resulting missionary emphasis. He complains of the general approach to the work of the Spirit by both Catholics and Protestants:

> In Roman Catholic theology, the Spirit is mainly the soul and sustainer of the Church. In Protestant theology he is mainly the awakener of individual spiritual life in justification and sanctification. So the Spirit is either institutionalized or individualized. And both of these opposite approaches are conceived in a common pattern of an introverted and static pneumatology. The Spirit in this way is the builder of the Church and the edifier of the

---

[1] Hendrikus Berkhof, *The Doctrine of the Holy Spirit*, 38
[2] Hendrikus Berkhof, *The Doctrine of the Holy Spirit*, 7.

faithful, but not the great mover and driving power on the way from the one to the many, from Christ to the world.[1]

Berkhof laments the neglect of the Spirit's work in mission, declaring that, "the Spirit, in bestowing his gifts upon men, is from the beginning aiming at their equipment for the great work of transmission."[2] Thus much weakness in pentecostal preaching can be attributed not only to the loss of content of the word—a result of dependence on the inner working of the Spirit apart from a systematic proclamation of the Gospel—but also an appropriation of anointed ministry for personal use that is sapping the Pentecostal Church of its power. Many examples could be cited; the need for healing or financial stability, for personal spiritual maturity—legitimate desires, yet misplaced if the motive is for personal comfort and not as a witness to the Gospel—which is the purpose of the gift of power of the Holy Spirit.

A less obvious example is the preacher who each week felt "burdened" by the Spirit and felt led to share that burden with his congregation. In fact, the "burden" was a reaction to difficulties in the assembly; his preaching agenda was set by these problems, and his proclamation of the word was sidetracked.[3] A loss of mission emphasis will deplete the anointing in preaching and will undermine its power.

## The Content is the Gospel

Jesus' own anointing was clearly in order to preach the Gospel, and that Gospel was freedom for those who heard.[4] The cardinal virtues of the Christian Faith are love, faith and hope,[5] and the primary goal of preaching must be to bring freedom and joy of reconciliation with God through these attributes.

---

[1] Hendrikus Berkhof, *The Doctrine of the Holy Spirit*, 33.
[2] Hendrikus Berkhof, *The Doctrine of the Holy Spirit*, 38.
[3] An example from personal experience.
[4] Luke 4:18–19.
[5] 1 Corinthians 13:13.

## Anointed Preaching

Recognizing this as the purpose of the anointing severely restricts the use of the pulpit from personal agendas, satisfaction of the pew, or even disputation about the finer points of doctrine[1] where these distract from proclamation of the Gospel to those in need. It is too easy to be seduced into preaching "another gospel," and consequently lose the power of the true Gospel—the Good News:

> The Gospel not only comes in power (1 Thessalonians 1:5) but *is* the power of God (Romans 1:16). It reveals the righteousness of God and leads to salvation to all who believe (Romans 1:16–17). Paul regards the Gospel as a sacred trust (1 Timothy 1:11). Thus he is under divine compulsion to proclaim it (1 Corinthians 9:16).[2]

Ramm indicates that the Bible is a means, not an end in itself. "The Bible is for one purpose: *to promote the spiritual prosperity of man*." He goes on to say:

> This is to say that the goal of all interpretation is *spiritual results* in the listeners. Hobart correctly says, "no man does good interpretation who does not look for results in men as the final aim of his interpretation."[3]

Elsewhere he reminds us that:

> The intention of Scripture is to supply man with the knowledge of salvation (2 Timothy 3:15), and what is necessary for a godly Christian life (2 Timothy 3:16–17). Only what is in some way related to these two themes is discussed in Scripture.[4]

---

[1] Correctly handling the word of truth obviously prohibits involvement in unnecessary controversies, 1 Timothy 1:3–7; 2 Timothy 2:14–15.

[2] L. D. Douglas, ed., *The New Bible Dictionary*. (Grand Rapids, Michigan IL: Eerdmans, 1962), 484

[3] Ramm, *Interpretation*, 96, his emphasis.

[4] Ramm, *Interpretation*, 180.

This idea seems so obvious, yet in practice frequently ignored for personal agendas, making complaints of the "Social Gospel" and liberal criticism of the text hypocritical. Preaching which in some measure does not proclaim the Gospel is illegitimate. Therefore, a clear understanding of what constitutes or contributes to the Gospel is a mandatory requirement of all preaching and preachers.

Jesus' anointing by the Spirit is the basis of our integrity to Scripture in preaching—he was anointed to preach the Gospel[1] and the gift of the Holy Spirit with power was given to be a witness to him.[2] That witness must reflect the Gospel of Jesus Christ or any claim of Spirit anointing is spurious. Therefore, a legitimate understanding of the final intention of Scripture must undergird any attempt at a valid pattern of anointed preaching.

Jesus' listeners noted that he spoke with authority.[3] They recognized the Jewish teachers did not. The teachers' "preaching" was not authentic because it lacked congruence with God's purposes, seen in Jesus. Jesus' mission was clear, to "preach the good news to the poor,"[4] and "I have not come to call the righteous, but sinners to repentance."[5] We do not have the same authority; ours, like the teachers of the law, is derived, and as such we speak with authority only as repeat his mission mediated through us by the Holy Spirit. Then our ministry will be authentic and with authority.

**The Centre is Christ**
In a review of some thirty works on preaching by Pentecostal authors, Byrd states that a:

---

[1] Luke 4:17–21. Note also the following: this was the intended ministry of the Servant of the Lord in Isaiah. 42:7, accomplished under the anointing of the Holy Spirit, Isaiah 61:1, and its performance confirmed, Luke 7:20–22.
[2] Acts 1:8.
[3] Matthew 7:28–29.
[4] Luke 4:18.
[5] Luke 5:31.

. . . Christocentric emphasis is shared by nearly every author of the pentecostal homiletical literature. The insistence upon Christocentric preaching is significant considering F. D. Bruner's theological critique of Pentecostalism.[1]

Bruner's critique endeavoured to match the theological problems in the Corinthian Church to the Pentecostals:

The features most prominent in first century Corinthianism are found to correspond to a remarkable degree with the features most distinctively present in twentieth century Pentecostalism.

This was in contrast to Paul whose "approach to this problem is thoroughly Christocentric," and Bruner lists Scriptures from Paul's Corinthian correspondence drawing the Corinthians to Christ.[2]

While few would dispute some extremism in the pentecostal movements, Fee's comment that "The issue at Corinth is one of correcting an abuse, not eliminating a nuisance,"[3] is the line most Pentecostals would take, using Paul's corrective as their guide. From personal experience, I agree with Byrd, that despite a high level of awareness of the Holy Spirit and frequent teaching concerning him, pentecostal preaching has always been the exaltation of Christ, rarely the exaltation of the Holy Spirit whose work is primarily to exalt Jesus Christ.

Of parallel interest in this issue is the Christocentric nature of New Testament hermeneutics. Longenecker, referring to the New Testament authors and their apparent lack of consciousness of exegetical genre or modes of interpretation, writes, as we noted earlier:

---

[1] Byrd, *Pentecostal Homiletic*, 84–85.
[2] Frederic Dale Bruner, *A Theology of the Holy Spirit.* (Grand Rapids MI: William B. Eerdmans, Publisher, 1970), 318.
[3] Fee, *Gospel and Spirit*, 99, n. 28.

What they were conscious of, however, is interpreting the Old Testament (1) from a Christocentric perspective, (2) in conformity with a Christian tradition, and (3) along Christological lines.[1]

Thus, whatever problems we may have in interpreting the New Testament authors' hermeneutics, we have little problem with the focus of their attention, the exaltation of Jesus Christ, who is the author, focus and end of the Gospel.

## THE NEED FOR FLEXIBILITY OF SERMON STYLE

**The Adopted Style**
Pentecostals have never felt bound to a particular sermon format, although Byrd shows that most Pentecostal preaching styles are "borrowed" from traditional homiletics:

> This adoption of traditional models is a result of upward economic and social status of the participants of the pentecostal movement. That is, as the movement's participants developed economically and socially, a stress for education for clergy was indicated by the rise of pentecostal Bible colleges. In terms of preaching models, the traditional deductive model was the primary model available and was readily "adopted."[2]

He uses the word "adoption" intentionally; the models were adopted wholesale without critical evaluation for "adaptation" suitable to the specific pentecostal tradition. Byrd reviews sermon styles specifically in order to attempt to create a style that reflects pentecostal belief and practice. As a result, he has detected "a gap between what the pentecostal sermon is

---

[1] Longenecker, "Can We Reproduce?" 16.
[2] Byrd, *Pentecostal Homiletic*, 112.

supposed to do in theory and the methods the preacher has to accomplish that function."[1]

There is a distinct parallel here with the hermeneutical shortcomings analyzed earlier. Because the "adopted" Pentecostal homiletic is based on rational models that focus on discovery of a propositional truth, there is no consideration for "re-experiencing" the text in a pentecostal context.[2] This idea of "re-experiencing the text" is to enable the audience to relive the experience of those recorded in the text; either mentioned in a specific narrative, or to whom a particular portion of Scripture was addressed. It is obvious that a variety of communication styles are going to accomplish this better that the traditional deductive models.

**A Proposed Alternate**

As a result, Byrd has endeavoured to track and build a homiletic style most suited to pentecostal expectations. His suggestion is the "sermonic plot" which attempts to "re-form" or "trans-form" the consciousness of the congregation. The plan is based on five steps: upset the equilibrium, analyze discrepancy, disclose clue, experience Gospel, and anticipate consequences.[3] Whatever its merits, probably its greatest drawback is that the style is not easy to understand and Byrd takes several pages to describe it in detail.[4]

While this method is specifically designed for anointed preaching, and as such may improve on the deductive method, the shortcoming of identifying a "suitable" pentecostal style is that it assumes not only that the Holy Spirit is more comfortable with a particular style, but also that all audiences have the same expectations. Even if argued that Byrd is specifically concerned with pentecostal audiences, his attempt still conflicts with the work

---

[1] Byrd, *Pentecostal Homiletic*, 107.
[2] Byrd, *Pentecostal Homiletic*, 112–113.
[3] Byrd, *Pentecostal Homiletic*, 233–234.
[4] Byrd, *Pentecostal Homiletic*, 231–240.

of the Spirit in the Acts record—Paul's speech on Mars hill differed dramatically from Peter's sermon on the day of Pentecost.

**Limitations of a Distinctive Style**
Certainly, a pentecostal homiletic needs a broader base than the traditional deductive model. In a similar vein to the rational rather than scriptural base for hermeneutics discussed in chapter two, the base sermonic form has been tied to Greek oratorical style, totally out of keeping with the variety of scriptural forms of preaching. Thus the deductive model is similarly unsuitable for the pentecostal desire to "re-experience" the text. But to simply replace it with another "suitable" model as Byrd suggests is simply moving the Holy Spirit from one straight-jacket to another.

This is not to imply that one's choice of style is unimportant simply because it is the Holy Spirit that makes the application. Diligence in providing a vehicle appropriate to the audience is important for the same reason as diligent study: to provide the best for the Spirit's use.

As the anointing of the Spirit should give greater insight into hermeneutics, so there should be a corresponding flexibility in sermon style, to reflect better the varied styles within Scripture, and also the format of Scripture itself. However, the content of preaching is not negotiable. The Holy Spirit can only be expected to honour the anointing as the preacher honours the stewardship of the Gospel entrusted to him.

## A REVIEW OF TRADITIONAL PENTECOSTAL STYLES

As mentioned earlier, Pentecostals have felt free to use a variety of sermon styles, although there has been a tendency to import evangelical styles into the movement. While this freedom has facilitated the level of Spirit inspiration that Pentecostals would consider necessary, it has not been without its drawbacks, particularly as lack of guidance provided grounds for something of a free for all.

**Traditional Categories Too Restrictive**
However, most responsible Pentecostals have recognized the need for providing legitimate vehicles for the transmission of the word to their congregations, and have codified some styles as appropriate. Byrd's review is helpful here, especially as the purpose of his book is to provide a pentecostal homiletic. His categories of current types are familiar to most, that of textual sermons taken generally from one text and used the most frequently; the topical sermon, and the expository.[1]

Byrd's general attitude is that "the categories are inadequate for pentecostal theology which emphasizes the importance of experiencing the biblical text in the contemporary situation."[2] Yet his understanding of the use of these sermon types is open to question. For example, he holds that, "The traditional categories of some sermons presuppose a hermeneutic that relates more of what a text 'meant,' that is, expository sermons expose the meaning of a passage."[3] Thus "the expository sermon is noted as one of the most difficult kind of sermons, but it is suggested as the 'best' kind of sermon."[4] This appears to assume that the expository sermon is more "difficult" because it is "encumbered" with too much Scripture which can inhibit direction, and thus is considered as commentary rather than preaching.

On the other hand, the textual sermon is the most commonly used, because it can be used too easily as a springboard for the preacher's ideas without limitations as to contextual meaning. Some typical pentecostal outlines contained in appendix four, can be used to illustrate this.

---

[1] Byrd, *Pentecostal Homiletic*, 110.
[2] Byrd, *Pentecostal Homiletic*, 112.
[3] Byrd, *Pentecostal Homiletic*, 112.
[4] Byrd, *Pentecostal Homiletic*, 111.

## Poor Pentecostal Understanding and Use of Categories

C. M. Ward's textual sermon, "A Tight Squeeze" in appendix four is suggested by the words "narrow place," but the sermon which follows has no relevance to the original meaning of the text which had to do with God's response to Baalam's disobedience. In fact, the text is never mentioned again and is irrelevant to the sermon. This is not to suggest that the sermon itself is not meaningful, but it needs to be built around a text that has more, if only indirect relevance, for instance, Matthew 7:13–14. But even here, the basic need is to derive the message from the text and context, not find a text to fit the message!

The pentecostal problem with expository sermons is well illustrated by G. Raymond Carlson's sermon "The Song of Salvation." Most Pentecostals would characterize expository preaching as the way this sermon is set out. It is long, and apart from the preacher, potentially boring in its "blow-by-blow" commentary. The use of wide-ranging Scriptures and complex thought can lose the average congregation, and the style is more of a selective teaching tool than a sermon. As a further caricature of expository preaching, it is almost purely cognitive, and there is no invitation for a response to the Gospel.

C. M. Ward's sermon, "Where Do You Go from Wit's End?" despite its single verse text, is a better example of expository preaching with content that a congregation can identify with. He uses and parallels the whole of Psalm 107:23–30, and finishes with an invitation that could well be built around verses 31–32. The dynamic of anointed preaching is not lost, but intensified by the proper use of expository means. However, does the sermon assume God will reverse or ameliorate the sufferer's circumstances? Without the full text we cannot be sure. If not, we can be sure God will take him or her through the difficulty, but our final prayer has to be: "Your will be done on earth as it is in heaven."[1]

**The Usefulness of a Varied Approach**
But while expository preaching is "safe"—it tends to ensure the message is biblical—other methods are equally, perhaps at times better suited to the work of the Holy Spirit in proclaiming the Gospel. Topical sermons which deal with contemporary needs can be effective if securely grounded in Scripture. Character studies are eminently scriptural,[2] and relevant on the basis that human nature does not change. Furthermore, for the informed preacher, character studies provide less opportunity for error, and the narrative style is easy listening.

In regard to narrative preaching, one that has received little attention is the parable—used frequently by the greatest of Spirit-anointed preachers. No doubt the history of the interpretation of Jesus' parables has been a tortured and unhappy one, yet the use of daily illustrations to picture the Gospel message is a powerful one. While Jesus "spoke plainly" at times to His disciples, his teaching to the others was primarily by way of the parable.

While there are theological problems with the reason for Jesus' parables[3] which is beyond the scope of this book, the use of the method need not be consequently proscribed: There are sermon suggestions almost everywhere if one has the eyes to see them. A preacher needs a sixth sense—the ability to see possibilities for sermons in his everyday experiences and reading.[4]

Lois Hauff's sermon "The White Elephant" would fall into this category. It is easy to imagine the genre; "The Kingdom of Heaven

---

[1] Matthew 6:10.
[2] Cf. for example the list of mentors in Hebrews 11, or those who failed, Hebrews 3:16–4:2, and 1 Corinthians. 10:1–13.
[3] For instance: were they meant to reveal or hide the truth? Cf. Matthew. 13:10–16.
[4] Leland R. Keys, "One Man's Methods," *Preparation for Preaching,* compiler Loius H. Hauff. (Available from the Central Bible College Library, Springfield MI.) 29.

is like a king whose servant owned a white elephant that was eating him out of house and home. The servant desired to sell the beast, but because of its religious significance . . . ." Despite its lack of a masthead text, and little coherent scriptural structure, the Gospel story comes through clearly and the opportunity for invitation is obvious.

Thus it must be clear that the content of the sermon is of far greater importance than the style. The anointing work of the Spirit depends on the faithfulness to the Gospel message, not the particular method of proclamation used.

**The Need for Simplicity**

There is also the question of the intellectual capability of the preacher. The disciples were unlearned, and to some current thinking used Scripture illegitimately yet successfully in spreading the Gospel. Can we support a hermeneutic that cannot be readily obtained from Scripture by the average informed Christian? Here we need to think also of the third world evangelist. Can we trust him to hermeneutics governed, or better, enlightened by the Holy Spirit? This is essential if those that God calls are going to be able to carry out their task. This does not preclude diligence, but affirms God's use of a person's meagre resources by the anointing of the Holy Spirit.

Here there is a distinct analogy with Roland Allen's classic thesis regarding the growth of the Christian Church. Written about 1927, Allen's book, *The Spontaneous Expansion of the Church*,[1] is concerned with the restrictive missionary methods of the early twentieth century Anglican Church, bound by its orders, but more particularly its fear for the doctrine. This led to a stifling of the natural zeal of new converts and a slow assimilation of indigenous people into the priesthood. He compares this with the attitude of the Early Church:

---

[1] Roland Allen, *The Spontaneous Expansion of the Church*. (Grand Rapids, MI: Eerdmans), 1962.

The Church of that day was apparently quite fearless of any danger that the influx of large numbers of what we should call illiterate converts might lower the standard of church doctrine. She held the tradition handed down by the apostles, and expected the new converts to grow up in it, to maintain it and to propagate it. And so in fact they did. The danger to the doctrine lay not in these illiterate converts on the outskirts; but at home in places like Ephesus and Alexandria, amongst the more highly educated and philosophically minded Christians. It was against these that she had to maintain doctrine.[1]

The latitude that Allen pleaded for in the furtherance of the Gospel must be available also for the Holy Spirit to perform his illuminating work in the field of preaching. The flexibility that is required is not necessarily an interpretation for all time, but must be one that allows the Holy Spirit to speak through the preacher to a specific need.

## SUMMARY

The Pentecostal Church has been known for its aggressive evangelism and its Christ-centred ministry as well as the emphasis on the empowering work of the Holy Spirit in the believer. However, the content of its preaching has at times left much to be desired, and a re-evaluation of its biblical base is necessary for the anointing of the Holy Spirit to continue. Particularly needed is a reverence for the scriptural text and a clearer exposition of it. Only here is the freedom typified by Jesus' anointing to be found, and genuine release experienced by the hearers.

While Pentecostals have developed a distinctive style of their own, preaching formats have by and large been adopted from

---

[1] Allen, *Spontaneous Expansion*, 48.

evangelical systems which may not always provide the best vehicle for anointed preaching, and often fall short of the methods used in the Bible. Pentecostals have a poor understanding of the purpose and use of the traditional formats, and have poorly adapted them to their own needs, or simply invented their own styles.

Pentecostal use of varied preaching styles is to be commended and encouraged, but needs to marry those styles to authentic Gospel proclamation.

# 4

## THE SIGNS OF ANOINTED PREACHING

> *I came to you in weakness and fear, and with much trembling. My message and my preaching were not with wise and persuasive words, but with a demonstration of the Spirit's power, so that your faith might not rest on men's wisdom, but on God's power.*
>
> *1 Corinthians 2:3–5*

Consistent with the pentecostal emphasis on experience, the pentecostal sermon has traditionally climaxed with some form of experiential response, frequently typified by the "altar service." This may often involve the gifts of the Spirit in operation, as well as baptism of the Holy Spirit, conversion and healing. These are generally accepted uncritically as evidence of the Spirit's presence, and in particular of his agreement with the word that has been proclaimed.

But this may not always be a certain means of discernment. In fact, there is much literature that claims that the "signs following" that are such an integral part of the pentecostal program can, in fact, be misleading. Thus the whole area of discernment and evidence of the Spirit's presence and work needs to be re-evaluated.

## THE NEED FOR EXPERIENCE

### An Intellectual Approach Insufficient

The pentecostal and charismatic movements have filled the void of Christian experience imposed by rationalist only theology, and this emphasis on the affective dimension of human experience is one of the reasons for the movements' growth through this century.[1] It is an anomaly of enormous proportions that modern theologians have, for the most part, insisted on an intellectual approach to faith. This is not only in the face of the need for a Spirit illuminated faith and against the trend towards spiritual experience in our society, but also against the trend of theologians and sceptics alike that empirical evidence alone cannot sustain faith.

This was true of sceptics like Hume, but also those who tried to rescue the faith. Kant had to base his "reason" on the moral imperative within, Schleiermacher on the sense of intuition apprehending the Infinite, and Hegel discovering meaning to life through the "World Spirit" working out his purposes in history. None of these methods effectively "saved" Christianity, for each of them reinterpreted Christianity from a purely intuitive sense. But at least they recognized the numinous quality of religion that needed to be apprehended by the affective before the cognitive gained understanding.

### Experience of Jesus Christ Prior to Understanding

The idea that "I believe, therefore I understand," rather than the rational reverse idea, is borne out in Colin Browne's search for an understanding of miracles:

---

[1] Paul G. Hiebert, "Discerning the Work of God," *Charismatic Experiences in History*, Cecil N. Robeck ed. (Peabody MA: Hendrickson Publishers, 1985), 48.

## Anointed Preaching

> For many of those who have come to believe in miracles, the question is not a three-step process, one that begins by establishing the existence and character of God on general grounds, then seeks to identify the God of the Bible with such a being, and finally fits Jesus and the miracles into this framework. It is more a matter of finding the miracle-working God of the Bible as the One who answers our deepest human needs in Jesus Christ. In such a case, the question of the existence of God is not logically prior to that of Jesus who works miracles.[1]

Our "deepest human needs" are rarely cognitive alone; for most barely cognitive at all, but a conviction of the truth deep within the human spirit placed there by the Spirit of God.

The view that the rational approach excluding experience is a valid hermeneutical stance can be carried over into preaching also. When denial of experience has been allowed to truncate understanding, it subsequently interferes with the anointing work of the Holy Spirit in the communication of the sermon. Not only is the experience of the listener important, but also the excitement of the preacher in his subject is imperative if his listeners are to be moved by his message. And his excitement is ignited by the illumination he receives from the Holy Spirit of the relevance of the word to him and his hearers' experience and need.

### The Experience of the Preacher

In pentecostal literature, prayer is noted most often as the primary means of sermon preparation, and is the "source of the anointing. . . . anointing comes from prayer, not study," although "the anointing gives insight and inspires the intellect for preparation."[2] Thus Pentecostals would hold that, the anointing of the Holy Spirit is not guaranteed every time for the pentecostal preacher, it must

---

[1] Colin Brown, *Miracles and the Critical Mind*. (Grand Rapids MI: Eerdmans Publishing Company, 1984), 285.
[2] Byrd, *Pentecostal Homiletic*, 76–77.

be sought in preparation for each sermon. While previous discussion notes that the anointing is resident on those called into service, it is also true that preaching is a crisis situation for the preacher requiring the special anointing of the Holy Spirit. John Piper claims that, "all genuine preaching is rooted in a feeling of desperation":

> You wake up on Sunday morning and you can smell the smoke of hell on one side and feel the crisp breezes of heaven on the other. You go to your study and look down at your pitiful manuscript, and you kneel down and cry, "God, this is so weak! Who do I think I am? What audacity to think that in three hours my words will be the odour of death to death and the fragrance of life to life. My God, who is sufficient for these things?"[1]

But in a major sense, preaching is also a crisis situation for all who listen. Their presence in the congregation is from felt or perceived need. They need, not only to hear a word of freedom and hope, but also to experience the intervention of God in their lives; one who deals with the whole person as Christ did on earth.

## The Experience of the Listener

Forbes, in recognising the need for spiritual experience, quotes from Louis Dupre's *Spiritual Life in a Secular Age*: "In our time, religious interpretation comes as a result of further reflection, and only rarely with the experience itself. Since the interpretation remains separate from the experience, the doubt about its correctness can be resolved only by a subsequent, full commitment to it." And, "The doctrines, lifestyles and methods of a previous age were conceived within the reach of a direct experience of the sacred. This has for the most part ceased to exist."[2]

---

[1] John Piper, *The Supremacy of God in Preaching*. (Grand Rapids MI: Baker Book House, 1990), 37–38.

[2] Forbes, *The Holy Spirit and Preaching*, 24.

## Anointed Preaching

If this is true, it is because those responsible for the deposit of faith and its proclamation have lost the sense of the Spirit in their preaching, and thus the Church as a whole has become correspondingly ineffective in its ministry. The experience of the pentecostal listener is both emotional and phenomenal. Most preachers recognize the need to approach the intellect, emotion and will, although many are afraid of stirring emotions. Yet it is clear from Scripture that the word in the hands of the Holy Spirit does affect the emotions also. Both intellect and emotions motivate the will.[1]

### THE EXPERIENCE OF SIGNS FOLLOWING

The distinctive tradition of pentecostal preaching has been with the Lord "confirming the word with signs following" of Mark 16:20. These signs centre on the signs promised in the previous verses, 17–18: driving out demons, speaking in new tongues, handling snakes and drinking poison without ill-effect, and the healing of the sick. While only extreme pentecostal groups advocate snake handling and poison drinking, the other signs generally fall into line with the gifts of the Holy Spirit mentioned elsewhere.[2] And Pentecostals generally would use this as an argument against the claim that the attestation of the end of Mark is too uncertain to be used as the basis for faith and life. In addition, conversion is also a sign confirming the Spirit's activity as exemplified following Peter's sermon on the Day of Pentecost.[3]

---

[1] Note for example weeping associated with the reading and understanding of the Law in Nehemiah 8:9, and the response to Peter's sermon on the Day of Pentecost, Acts 2:37.

[2] E.g. The gifts listed in 1 Corinthians 12:7–10, and the practice of the New Testament missionaries, Acts 14:3.

[3] Acts 2:41.

## The Altar Service

In the "altar service," a feature of most pentecostal churches, the expectation of signs is formalised. This is the place of both the "Kleenex" box, and the disowned crutch; the place of conviction and healing, of both need and supply. It is a place of active response to the Gospel and "confirming of the word with signs following." The call for response following a sermon is an integral part of the message and cannot be separated from it, and generally takes the form of a call to the front of the church or to an adjacent prayer room. This call is foremost for those seeking salvation, but is also frequently broadened to any experiencing a specific need.

This responsive type of ministry was made popular by Charles Finney in the 1820s, when he "brought revival methods into an ordered pattern which became known as the 'new measures.'" These measures, which included "inquiry meetings and the 'anxious bench'—were not really new, of course. It was the shaping of them into a system designed to produce results that was the novel feature." This raised "the opposition of those who feared the emotionalism of frontier and 'new measures' evangelism."[1]

Lloyd-Jones recognized the need to provide balance between:

> . . . two great principles laid down in the New Testament for our help and guidance. . . . The first principle is that everything must be done decently and in order (1 Corinthians 14:40). But there is another statement: "Quench not the Spirit" (1 Thessalonians 5:19).[2]

Most churches have little problem with the first principle. But adherence only to that ensures that "everything is perfectly controlled, everything is nice, orderly, correct, formal, and above all respectable":

---

[1] Williston Walker, *A History of the Christian Church*. (New York NY: Charles Scribner's Sons, third edition 1970), 508.

[2] D. Martyn Lloyd-Jones, *Revival*, (Westchester IL: Crossway Books, 1987), 73.

You will always observe that when forms of service become formal, the Spirit is less in evidence, and you move further away from the New Testament. The very characteristic of the New Testament Church was this spontenaity, this life, this living quality, this vivacity. But as you fall away from the Spirit and his influence, everything becomes formal. So you have forms of service. You will find that the Church in every period of declension becomes much more formal in her services, she adopts forms of service and she tends to turn to liturgy, and to ritual.[1]

But the opposite danger are the issues of "confusion," "excitement"—a false sense of joy—and "emotionalism," each of which brings the Gospel into disrepute. In commenting that revivals are always subject to these charges, Lloyd-Jones adds, "And that is why the New Testament tells us to prove all things, and to hold fast only to that which is good."[2]

So it is not unexpected that at this point Pentecostals have been criticized for emotional manipulation, for there is a fine line between emotionalism and conviction. If Pentecostals are to be criticized justly, it is that they have formalised the Spirit-given emotional response to the point at which the expectation of it prompts emotional manipulation to ensure it. It is not uncommon, unfortunately for emotions to be stirred with a heart-wrenching story or "guilt-tripping" which ultimately has little in common with the hope and freedom proclaimed by the Gospel. Thus, the emotional appeal can become liturgy, and in so doing, falls into the error of both extremes at the same time. It is the fear of this that causes Lloyd-Jones to comment:

> . . . that in our fear of emotionalism, some of us may be in grave danger of banishing emotions altogether. Oh, there

---

[1] Lloyd-Jones, *Revival*, 76.
[2] Lloyd-Jones, *Revival*, 75.

may be plenty of sentiment, but I am not talking about sentiment. Sentiment is weak and flabby. Sentiment is that which a hard man puts on to persuade himself that he still has some feeling within him. No. we do not want sentiment, sickly, maudlin sentiment, we want emotion, that God-given quality. When did you last weep because of your distance from God? Some of us have forgotten how to weep, my friends. When did we last weep for joy, out of sheer joy and the sense of the glory of God? Many of us are afraid of emotions.[1]

How is that emotion evoked? Lloyd-Jones adds, "The emotions are to be approached through the understanding, through the mind, by truth."[2] The necessity for authoritative content cannot be evaded, it is the only legitimate route of conviction.

## The Problem of Discernment

This expectation gives rise to two problems for the pentecostal preacher. The first is practical; there is a pressure of expectation placed upon him for a display of the gifts of the Spirit, or the alternate possibility that his preaching is not "anointed." This, in turn, intensifies the second problem that he faces: discerning of the genuineness or source of the manifestations and the tendency not to look too closely at the manifestations that "confirm" his ministry.

Thus it is here that a real danger exists. The importance of "signs following" for the Pentecostal has led to the seduction of many to "another gospel,"[3] and to aberrant expressions of the faith such as the "Prosperity Gospel" and the "Kingdom Now" movements. This need for signs, together with a mistaken idea of what constitutes "holy boldness," addressed later in this chapter,

---

[1] Lloyd-Jones, *Revival*, 78.
[2] Lloyd-Jones, *Revival*, 75.
[3] Cf. the work of Don R. McConnell, *A Different Gospel.* (Hendrickson Publishers, Peabody, Massachusetts, 1995), regarding the Word-Faith movement.

has also led others to follow television evangelists of doubtful reputation, even after their exposure.

The difficulty with signs is twofold. Jesus apparently used signs to authenticate his ministry,[1] and yet both he and the New Testament attribute miraculous signs to unbelievers and to Satan himself:

> To open the door for the involvement of the spiritual dimension in human affairs is to allow the Holy Spirit to work more effectively in our lives. It also opens the door to the rulers and the powers of darkness. What God does, Satan counterfeits. This is clear in Scripture for we are constantly warned about false prophets, false signs and wonders, and false teachings (Colossians 2:8; 1 Timothy 4:1–2; 2 Timothy 4:3). It should not surprise us, therefore, that the charismatic movement, like all movements before it, must face the possibilities of distortion.[2]

Second, Jesus denied signs to those who required them, in fact he called those who asked for a sign "a wicked and adulterous generation," and left them only the "sign of the prophet Jonah," a reference to his death and resurrection.[3] A fresh understanding of the place and purpose of signs following authentic preaching content by Pentecostals, is necessary if the movement is to retain its founding principles.

**The Dubious Sources of Signs**

That Pentecostals should be led easily astray is a paradox, when one of the gifts of the Holy Spirit is that of discernment, the distinguishing between spirits.[4] Yet on the basis of what we have seen so far this should not be a surprise, for the Spirit works with

---

[1] Note that in Luke 7:18–23, Jesus authenticates his ministry to John the Baptist by works prophesied in his commission, Luke 4:18–19.
[2] Hiebert, "Discerning," 150.
[3] Matthew 12:39; 16:4; Mark 8:12; Luke 11:29–30.
[4] 1 Corinthians 12:10.

the word, and as the word is the final arbiter of correct teaching and experience, so the word is the yardstick by which the Holy Spirit guides discernment of the spirit behind the sign. The less biblically literate the believer is, the less the resource available to the Spirit to protect him or her.

Here then is the crux of the problem. The signs are not themselves the test of the Holy Spirit's work. Rather, the source of the signs is to be discerned. As Heibert points out:

> Many Christians use particular phenomenological criteria to test the presence of the Holy Spirit, for these are easily applied. Some look for glossalalia, others for healings, miracles, ecstatic experiences and resurrections from the dead. But all of these are found in the other major religions of the world and in tribal animism.[1]

Heibert goes on to describe various examples of "signs:"in a variety of religious settings, including the use of the name of Jesus Christ,[2] and concludes, "there are in fact, no simple phenomenological criteria by which we can test the presence of the Holy Spirit."[3]

Hermann Gunkel wades into this area by listing both similarities and differences between the work of demons and the Holy Spirit. Similarities caused confusion among the observers; generally malicious or unresponsive Jews insisted that Jesus had a demon. Even John the Baptist appeared confused, and both Paul and John had to exhort their congregations to test the spirits.[4] Gunkel lists further similarities: inward residence of both the Holy Spirit and demons; words spoken could be the Spirit or demons

---

[1] Heibert, "Discerning," 150.
[2] Even Jesus warned of the misuse of His Name, Matthew 7:22–23. Cf. also Acts 19:13–16. The Acts passage suggests that not all who used the name of Jesus suffered the same fate as Sceva's sons.
[3] Hiebert, "Discerning," 151.
[4] Hermann Gunkel, *The Influence of the Holy Spirit: the Popular View of the Apostolic Age and the Teaching of the Apostle Paul*, tr. by Roy A. Harrisville and Philip A. Quanbeck II. (Philadelphia PN: Fortress Press, 1979), 49.

speaking; both exhibited superhuman knowledge, and there were similarities between being Spirit-driven and demon possessed.[1] According to Gunkel, much of the Jewish confusion was attributable to the Old Testament idea of an "evil spirit from the Lord."[2]

Differences set out by Gunkel included the greater power of Jesus, the name of Christ as Lord, and the perniciousness of demons.[3] However, his ideas do not carry weight. The measure of greater power is subjective, Gunkel recognizes the subjectiveness of the viewers "according to the temper of the one who passes judgement."[4] The perniciousness of the demons is not always discernible, they might deceive even the elect,[5] and we have already seen that the use of the name of Jesus is no guarantee of the Spirit's presence.

**The Basis of Discernment**
However, in his short essay, Hiebert suggests some possibilities for discernment: agreement with Scripture, maturity and the fruit of the Spirit, balance, unity and what he calls wholism—the recognition of God's working in all of life, not just the miraculous.[6]

But of more interest are other ideas in his essay, that of the Lordship of Christ, and affirmation by the faith community at large. Taking the latter point first, the one who prophesied in the church was accountable to the congregation at large:

> . . . "the others weigh carefully what is said." [1 Corinthians 14:29] This latter item is the verb for "distinguishing between spirits" in 1 Corinthians 12:10. As noted there, this is probably to be understood as a form of

---
[1] Gunkel, *The Influence of the Holy Spirit*, 50-51.
[2] Gunkel, *The Influence of the Holy Spirit*, 53.
[3] Gunkel, *The Influence of the Holy Spirit*, 54-55.
[4] Gunkel, *The Influence of the Holy Spirit*, 40.
[5] Matthew 24:24.
[6] Heibert, "Discerning," 154-159.

"testing the spirits," but not so much in the sense of whether "the prophet" is speaking by a foreign spirit but whether the prophecy itself truly conforms to the Spirit of God, who is also indwelling the other believers.[1]

While the preacher is not to be identified with the prophet, nevertheless his anointing and illumination by the Holy Spirit requires his affirmation or otherwise by the other listening believers. In other words, the discernment must begin with the content of the preacher's message before (in terms of priority) signs are manifested.

The other test, that of the Lordship of Christ, also begins with the preacher's message, but also has to do with the meaning of the signs which may be manifest. Colin Brown debates this issue at length and he claims that the rules governing prophets, Deuteronomy 13:1–5, and 18:22, were the basis of Jewish interpretation of signs and miracles. Thus, to the Jews who viewed these miracles they rejected Jesus' claim as the Son of God, Messiah, because His miracles were seen as those of a common magician or false prophet designed to seduce the people. Brown explains:

> Moreover if Jesus had performed a sign, he would have walked straight into a trap. For a sign could readily have been construed as none other than the work of Beelzebul. Matthew's temptation story tells of Satanic enticements to perform such signs (4:1–11). The temptations were temptations to use the power of the Spirit for selfish ends, and to gain a following by means of impressive but non-redemptive signs. However, the student of the Law knew full well that signs were at best inconclusive and at worst incriminating evidence of magic and the occult. They required that the person who wrought the sign should be

---

[1] Gordon Fee, *The First Epistle to the Corinthians*. (Grand Rapids MI: Eerdmans Publishing Co., 1987), 693.

put to death (Deuteronomy 13), so that the evil would be purged out of the midst of the people.[1]

The obvious question then follows: what was the point of the miracles if their evidence was inconclusive? The answer to this question has necessary relevance for the understanding of the pentecostal claim of signs following. In fact, the scriptural reference to "signs" following and not "miracles" contains the basis of the answer. In response to the conflict between signs freely given, and others denied by Jesus, Brown says: "But these were signs for those who believed the Law and the Prophets and sought to understand Jesus from that perspective. To the evil and adulterous generation no sign would be given except the sign of the prophet Jonah."[2] If there was to be any conclusive miracle it would be the resurrection of Jesus from the dead, typified by the story of Jonah. Yet even this failed and still fails to convince against unbelief.[3]

## Signs are Pointers, Not Proofs

Brown concludes that the miracle stories were not intended to provide proofs of Jesus' divinity nor the authenticity of his teaching:

> But a sign is not the same as a proof. It is never free from ambiguity. It is a pointer, an indication. As such, it falls short of conclusive demonstration. The miracles recorded in the Gospels serve as indicators, summoning a response of insight, faith, and obedience.[4]

On this basis, signs may awaken faith, but its final object is not in the miracle, but is Jesus himself. The signs become incidental once they have done their work in pointing to Jesus. Further, the

---

[1] Brown, *Miracles*, 313.
[2] Brown, *Miracles*, 314.
[3] Luke 16:27–31.
[4] Brown, *Miracles*, 286.

emphasis is on the Lordship of Jesus Christ, and not on the miracle, the personal comfort of the recipient, nor the curiosity of the onlooker. The pentecostal preacher who is truly anointed will not seek signs following his preaching, but concentrate on Jesus Christ and his Gospel. While he may consider signs following possible, or even probable, he will advocate them only as incidentally contributing to the proclamation of the Gospel, and the response of faith of his hearers.

## THE PARADOX OF POWER: ITS FOUNDATION OF WEAKNESS

It would appear that for many pentecostal preachers the concept of power in the New Testament has been completely misconstrued. A desire to see the power of the Holy Spirit displayed has overridden the prior concepts that are a prerequisite. Yet the relationship between personal weakness and the appropriation of spiritual power pervades the teaching of the New Testament. The areas of Scripture where this concept is most prevalent are reviewed in appendix three.

### The Need of Weakness

Again, as with the work of the Holy Spirit in preaching, little has been written on this subject in preaching manuals, although Martyn Lloyd-Jones has given some insight. In a passage dealing with the evidences of the call of the preacher, he says:

> But let us check it yet further by something which is equally important. I have hinted at it already, and that is, that there is in you a sense of diffidence, a sense of unworthiness, a sense of inadequacy. No more perfect expression of this can be found anywhere than in 1 Corinthians 2, where Paul talks about "weakness, fear, and much trembling."[1]

---
[1] Lloyd-Jones, *Preachers*, 106.

Baumann contributes half a page to humility, recognizing it as a virtue in the preacher on the basis that God chose the weak and despised to proclaim the Gospel.[1] Stott has noted this truth and opened the door to the danger and the remedy of boldness in the pulpit:

> Unfortunately, the resolve to be courageous in the pulpit can result in our becoming headstrong and arrogant. We may succeed in being outspoken, but spoil it by becoming proud of our outspokenness. Truth to tell, the pulpit is a perilous place for any child of Adam to occupy. It is "high and lifted up", and thus enjoys a prominence which should be restricted to Yahweh's throne (Isaiah 6:1). . . . Pride is without doubt the chief occupational hazard of the preacher. It has ruined many, and deprived them of their ministry of power.[2]

He adds, "In order to receive his power, we first have to admit, and then even to revel in, our own weakness."[3] It is the emphasis on power, despite its legitimacy, but without recognizing the New Testament's emphasis on the necessity of human weakness, which has contributed most to the disgrace of some Pentecostal pulpits. Stott reviews the need of the Corinthian church, and similar statements could be true of segments of today's pentecostal movement and of individual churches:

> It is this last paradox, which, I confess, has struck me most among all the varied ways in which the New Testament authors express the same truth. "Power through weakness": it is a recurring theme, perhaps even the dominant theme, in Paul's Corinthian correspondence. The Corinthians badly needed it too. For they were a proud

---

[1] Baumann, *Contemporary Preaching*, 41.
[2] John R. W. Stott, *Between Two Worlds, The Art of Preaching in the Twentieth Century.* (Grand Rapids, MI: Eerdmans Publishing Co., 1982), 320.
[3] Stott, *Between Two Worlds*, 330.

people, boastful of their gifts and attainments on the one hand, and boastful of their leaders on the other, indulging in a disgraceful personality cult, playing one apostle off against another, in a way that horrified Paul.[1]

In endeavouring to come to terms with this paradox, "power through weakness," Stott paraphrases three passages from the Corinthian correspondence. In them he draws attention to the use of the Greek *hina*, "in order that," to better indicate the dependence of power on weakness. These are his paraphrases:

> I was with you in personal weakness, and therefore relied on the Holy Spirit's powerful demonstration of the truth of my message, *in order that* your faith might rest in God's power alone. (1 Corinthians 2:3–5)

Again:

> We have the treasure of the gospel in fragile earthenware pots (that's how weak and brittle our bodies are), *in order that* it may be plainly seen that the tremendous power which sustains us and converted you comes from God and not from ourselves. (2 Corinthians 4:7)

In addition:

> Because Jesus told me that his power is made perfect in human weakness, therefore I will gladly boast about my weaknesses, *in order that* Christ's power may rest on me. . . . For it's only when I'm weak that I'm strong. (2 Corinthians 12:7–10)[2]

Until the preacher has come face to face with his own weakness, and has learned to live with a sense of his own desperate need for God's power to fulfil the work of the ministry, he will not experience the real power of the Holy Spirit. It seems that the

---

[1] Stott, *Between Two Worlds*, 330.
[2] Stott, *Between Two Worlds*, 331.

## Anointed Preaching

power of the Spirit is available in direct proportion to the recognition of the individual's need and dependence upon Him, and in inverse proportion to the individual's sense of ability and self reliance. The weakness of the preacher is not a virtue to be sought, or worse, to exult in. It is a reflection and sign of the weakness of the One who deliberately laid aside his glory to become a man and share human weakness and death.[1] His power revealed in our weakness demonstrates the power released in Jesus' own weakness.

### The Basis of Weakness

Yet even Stott appears to miss the point of the passages. He suggests that "human weakness was deliberately permitted to continue, in order to be the medium through which divine power could operate", and then catalogues recent giants of the faith whose handicaps contributed to a "triumphant vindication of the transcendent independence of the Spirit over the handicap of the body."[2] Fee, however, senses the parabolic nature of the passages in his commentary on 1 Corinthians 2:1-5:

> At the heart of [Paul's] preaching stood the "weakness of God" (1:25), the story of a crucified Messiah (2:2). His own weaknesses served as a further visible demonstration of the same message, but even more to demonstrate that the message was of divine, not human, origin (see especially 2 Corinthians 4:7 and 13:4). Thus the apostle regularly glories in his weaknesses, not because he "enjoyed ill health" but because they were a sure evidence that the power was of God and not of himself.[3]

Thus:

---

[1] Philippians 2:5-8
[2] Stott, *Between Two Worlds*, 331–332.
[3] Fee, *First Corinthians*, 93.

Even the preacher whom God has used to bring them to faith had to reject self-reliance. One senses that for Paul this is not merely a historical replay of his time with them, but also functions as something of a paradigm for his understanding of Christian ministry, a paradigm that will be spelled out in greater detail in 4:11–13 and especially in 2 Corinthians. 2:14 to 6:13.[1]

## THE SIGN OF THE FRUIT OF THE SPIRIT

### The Lack in Pentecostal Literature

Perhaps this lack of understanding of the real meaning of dependence has occasioned the glaring gap in pentecostal homiletics: that of the relevance of fruit of the Spirit to preaching. Neither Forbes nor Byrd mention the fruit of the Spirit in their dissertations, and Byrd's work includes a review of some thirty pentecostal authors on preaching published at the time of this writing. This seems a strange omission from a movement dedicated to the work of the Holy Spirit.

And yet on further reflection perhaps this omission is a tacit admission that the fruit of the Spirit with its self-effacing character is an embarrassment to a movement primarily dedicated to the experience of the power of God through the Holy Spirit. But, as we have seen, the character of the fruit of the Spirit is not at all at odds with his power. Although there appears to be little or no literature on this area, power and authority in the pulpit is in fact dependent on the fruit of the Holy Spirit, and pulpit authority needs to be viewed using the fruit of the Spirit as one of the factors of discernment.

### Character Mistakenly Viewed as Ethical

Byrd does tackle the character of the preacher, addressing both the spiritual and ethical character. Neither of these categories are

---

[1] Fee, *First Corinthians*, 90.

## Anointed Preaching

viewed from a broad scriptural viewpoint, again despite Byrd's review of a number of pentecostal authors. Spiritual formation consists of a "call" confirmed by others, and by the inward witness of the Spirit, and the Spirit's anointing to enhance the preacher's faculties. C. L. Allen also requires the preacher's baptism in the Holy Spirit, and speaking in tongues.[1] Allen is further quoted in regard to the preacher's character:

> It has long been my personal conviction that the preparation of the man, both as to his personal character and to his spiritual life, is far more important and necessary to his success as a pentecostal preacher. I am not minimizing the importance of the message. What I am saying is that it is more important to prepare the man than it is to prepare the message. My reason for saying this is that people will read the man more than they will read the message, they will see the man more than they will see the message, and they will hear the man more than they will hear the message.[2]

Allen is saying here "The medium is the message." But whatever the initial speaking in tongues may signify, it is not a measure of Christian growth, rather an evidence of the grace of God. Spiritual formation depends more on the fruit of the Spirit—the growth to Christ-likeness, than on the gifts of the Spirit. Evidence of the anointing of the Spirit of God on a preacher in both his life and his pulpit ministry must be seen from this perspective.

But most of the material Byrd reviews generally uses moral categories to establish the integrity of the preacher. Much of this has its roots in both the Wesleyan Holiness and non-Wesleyan evangelical doctrines of sanctification, the former believing in instant sanctification as a second work of grace, the other in a

---

[1] Byrd, *Pentecostal Homiletic*, 90–91.
[2] Byrd, *Pentecostal Homiletic*, 91.

progressive view.[1] Little is written about the scriptural categories of standards for preachers. From various sources Byrd cites love, loyalty, devotion, accountability, integrated pulpit and life ministry and sexual fidelity. Negative standards to be avoided are arrogance, "professionalizing" the ministry, desire for luxury, attitudes of jealousy and frivolousness. Within the pulpit, there are also constraints; confidences must not be betrayed or personal matters discussed, and unsympathetic or fearful attitudes are to be avoided.[2]

While much of this is to be commended, and preachers should at least meet the standards of the society in which they practise, an aim for a well-documented spiritual maturity is primarily required. The preacher anointed by the Holy Spirit must show signs of the scriptural foundations for integrity and maturity, the basis of which must be the fruit of the Spirit.

**The Process of Spiritual Formation**
On this issue Forbes, despite his omission of the fruit of the Spirit, does deal with the anointing as a process of spiritual formation as well as a repetitive experience. He has identified ten dimensions of the anointing work of the Holy Spirit in the life of Jesus. He is not intending to provide "some exact formula. The intention is to call attention to specific aspects of Jesus' development so that we can use these insights for enriching our understanding of spiritual formation."[3]

He list these insights as (1) Jesus' unique relationship with his heavenly parent, (2) nurture by his family and family of faith, (3) reaching the point of vocational readiness, and (4) obedience to baptism upon impulse of the Spirit. (5) Jesus experienced sacramental grace—the experience of baptism, (6) divine approval, acceptance and appointment, (7) and power beyond himself. 8) He

---

[1] Byrd, *Pentecostal Homiletic*, 92.
[2] Byrd, *Pentecostal Homiletic*, 92–95.
[3] Forbes, *The Holy Spirit and Preaching*, 38.

was tested in the wilderness, (9) experienced the ministry of angels, and (10) demonstrated strength to bear witness to his community of faith.[1]

Byrd is intensely critical of Forbes at this point. In one of the few critical passages of Byrd's dissertation, he views Forbes strictly through the lens of pentecostal doctrine and experience, suggesting that Forbes is denying the definition of experience given by Jesse Moon.[2] It is unfortunate that Byrd appears at this point as an apologist for traditional pentecostal dogma, rejects the wider and congruent work of the anointing of the Holy Spirit, and thus has nothing to say to the wider community of faith.

There is little doubt about the place of experience in the Christian life. Discussion about experience must centre on its limits and validation, not on its validity. The need of experience as a necessary adjunct to intellectual understanding has fueled the pentecostal and charismatic movements which have filled this void during the past century.

Validation of that experience, and its manifestations is the crux of the present task of Pentecostals. As the last chapter indicated the need for responsible biblical preaching to reflect the Gospel, so this chapter has revealed the need to rethink and discern more clearly signs of the Spirit's presence in the various manifestations expected in the pentecostal sphere.

But also there must be a clearer understanding of the relationship of the fruit of the Spirit in the life and preaching of the preacher. Power is available only as a resource to fill the void of perceived and desperate inadequacy within the Christian, and this is of comparably greater significance in the preacher who is anointed to preach the Gospel with power.

---

[1] Forbes, *The Holy Spirit and Preaching*. 37–38.
[2] Byrd, *Pentecostal Homiletic*, 76, n 40. Byrd recognizes Forbes' agreement with Moon, but assumes that Forbes' process is incompatible with it.

## SUMMARY

The pentecostal emphasis on experience has been a necessary and welcome corrective to counter the rational cognitive basis of most evangelicalism, although most Pentecostals are aware of the dangers of emotionalism. While the previous chapter has dealt with the tendency to rely on Spirit inspired conviction to the detriment of clear proclamation of the word, this chapter has dealt with the other potential problem of experienced based ministry—that of dependence on signs.

The pentecostal desire for signs following, while scriptural, is full of pitfalls awaiting the inexperienced and uninformed. The need here for re-evaluation is necessary. Like anointed preaching, the misuse and misunderstanding of signs following should not result in a shelving of the issue, but a careful review of their place and use for the future.

Allied to signs following is the idea of power in the pulpit. Again the dangers are not always apparent, but Scripture gives clear teaching on the place of power, and its corollary the need for the self-effacing nature of Christianity. This humility is clearly described in the fruit of the Spirit, which must be a major part of the Pentecostal's pneumatology.

## CONCLUSION

Although most agree on the essential work of the Holy Spirit in preaching, we have seen that little research has been done in this area. I have attempted to show that not only is the Holy Spirit's work in preaching mostly recognized, but also that it can be identified and fostered by the preaching ministry. That work of the Spirit in preaching is clearly his anointing ministry—frequently misused by Pentecostals, and mostly ignored and discarded by the rest.

Yet among non-Pentecostals, the anointing presence has been acknowledged, but mostly viewed with scepticism and avoided for fear of being seduced by the unknown. On the other hand, many who are ignorant of the Spirit's working or dispute the pentecostal claim, will often exhibit an anointing on their preaching, and render a powerful and convicting ministry.

Byrd has attempted to systematize the understanding of pentecostal preaching, in order to produce a pentecostal homiletic. Consequently he has focussed his attention on pentecostal doctrine and practice, and has had little to say to his evangelical brothers. This is unfortunate, for anointed preaching cannot be retained within the Pentecostal Church any more than the burgeoning evangelical scholarship can eventually be kept out.

Forbes however, has sensed the power in anointed preaching, not just as a passing phenomenon, but as an essential part of the ministry of the wider Church. He has recognized the potential of preachers of all communions who have both a depth of Bible knowledge and an empowering Spirit anointed ministry, and he has attempted to broaden that ministry for all evangelical fellowships.

Pentecostals do not have an exclusive claim on the Holy Spirit and his anointing ministry; in fact, their desire is that all may share his fullness. He is not boxed into anybody's system, nor is he kept out by their elaborate defences. What is more to the point, Pentecostals have not only areas of the anointing ministry to learn, they also need to recall some things that they appear to have forgotten. But despite their shortcomings, they also have much to teach.

Probably because of their experience orientation, Pentecostals have an intuitive feel for the anointing of the Spirit on preaching, and for the wider use of scriptural genres than the more conservative rationalists would allow. This cannot be discounted because of the mistakes they may have made; the mistakes are made because they have been willing to open themselves to the Spirit even at the risk of error.

The work presently being done in the area of hermeneutics must continue. The pentecostal message cannot exist within the artificial restraints that rational interpreters would place it. Although pentecostals have rarely felt constrained in this area, honest research to validate their stance must continue if pentecostal ministry is to have integrity. As Gordon Fee says: . . . my long experience in evangelical settings makes me urge that we articulate our hermeneutics in such a way that these friends will find it at least viable, if not always compelling.[212]

Pentecostals have provided a place for both experience and emotion in the faith, and so have met people where they live—a preaching ministry to the whole person, so that God can reach the whole person. But, of course, it is not intuition, but God himself through his Holy Spirit who has opened their minds and hearts to his fullness. And they do produce hearable sermons!

---

[212] Fee, *Gospel and Spirit*, 104.

But if Pentecostals are to regain their position as a force for the penetration of the Gospel into our culture, they also have to learn, in some cases relearn, some basic lessons. Their sermons must re-establish a clear Gospel content built upon a dedicated understanding of the Bible. This means being open to evangelical scholarship so readily available. There is no excuse today for ignorant or casual handling of God's word in North America. But, there is room for broadening the sermon base and understanding the uses to which they can be put. Here, Pentecostals have had a wider base than Evangelicals generally, but a better understanding of those used elsewhere would strengthen their search for pertinent content.

Of critical importance is the re-evaluation of the understanding of "signs following," and the source of spiritual power. Being hung-up on signs can be both a distraction from the Gospel and Christ as the centre, but also a deceptive ploy of spirit forces, or common charlatans. A more mature knowledge of the place of signs would not only assist in avoiding deception, it would also foster their legitimate use.

Finally, a movement so involved in the work of the Holy Spirit must come to a better understanding of the place of the fruit of the Spirit in life and ministry. A sense of personal acquisition of spiritual power and power tripping, has undermined many a promising ministry, and spells disaster for evangelism and attempts at building strong churches.

Implementing change is never easy. But change must come if the pentecostal movement is to maintain its cutting edge; perhaps in some cases even survive. On-the-job training for those already in ministry should be as acceptable as similar training in secular fields, and for greater reasons. Not only are we living in a rapidly changing society, but we are all subject to the temptations from our adversary that distract us from legitimate ministry of the word.

But long term change will eventually come through the Bible colleges where future ministers are to be trained. Pentecostals can no longer isolate themselves; co-operation with other colleges can be an asset to both communions. For example, Central Bible College in Saskatoon has had an integrative program with a local Lutheran college for several years and other pentecostal colleges have followed.

Ideas of distinctive pentecostal preaching can be, and need to be, rethought and taught, rather than opting to discard them. But they need to be integrated with an understanding of the fruit of the Spirit as Christian virtues to be sought and cherished. The ideas of expository and other forms of biblical preaching commendably aimed for in pentecostal colleges must not be taught without a clear understanding of the anointing work of the Holy Spirit, which has provided the Pentecostals with their power.

The two strands apparent in the movement today need not be mutually exclusive as they are often assumed to be. There is no way to go back to the "good old days." They have gone forever. We have to minister in the world as it is today, with the Spirit's resources for today's world. But neither can Pentecostals with integrity leave behind the anointed preaching that gave them their dynamism.

The movement that eventually combines a respect for the word of God, with the anointing power of the Holy Spirit in its preaching ministry will be the movement that again sees God's dynamic action in its world and beyond.

# APPENDICES

Bryan Norford

# APPENDIX 1

## A REVIEW OF THE SCRIPTURAL SIGNIFICANCE OF ANOINTING

The Old Testament idea of anointing is translated from the Hebrew and its derivatives, and in its natural sense referred to the applying of oil to a shield[1] or the body,[2] or even painting a house.[3] For religious purposes, tabernacle or temple objects were also anointed,[4] possibly following the example set by Jacob's anointing of the stone at Bethel with oil.[5]

The following references denote both actual physical anointing, but also the Spirit of God coming down upon many, representing an anointing by God. Several Old Testament references indicate both, and many New Testament references indicate anointing signified by the coming of the Holy Spirit on the recipient. For our purposes, the anointing of persons is relevant, and the Old Testament clearly cites a pattern of anointing of people for God's service by the pouring of designated anointing oil over the head.[6] Men were anointed specifically for service in a variety of functions, as artisans,[7] judges,[1] kings,[2] priests[3] and prophets.[4] prophets.[4]

---

[1] Isaiah 21:5.
[2] Amos 6:6.
[3] Jeremiah 22:14.
[4] Exodus 30:22–29.
[5] Genesis 28:18, 31:13.
[6] Francis Brown et al. *Hebrew and English Lexicon*. (Oxford: Clarendon Press, 1980), 603, see also Psalm 133:2.
[7] Exodus 28:3; 31:3; 35:31.

Victor Hamilton suggests a fourfold theological significance of anointing in the Old Testament.[5] Firstly, anointing signified a separation for God's service, with a correspondingly increased accountability.[6] Secondly, though the anointing agent was human, the Lord was understood as the authorizing agent, indicating that the anointed one was inviolable and to be held in high regard,[7] and thirdly, that the anointing was accompanied with divine enablement;[8] the coming of the Holy Spirit upon them with power. Finally, the development of the idea of a coming Messiah, *meshiah*,—Anointed One—is increasingly discernible in the Old Testament.[9] Although anointing is not mentioned, it is implicit in the coming of the Spirit upon the seventy elders in the record of Moses extremity,[10] and on the Prophets Elijah and Elisha.[11]

In the New Testament, the verb *chrino*—to anoint—only occurs five times, three of which refer to Jesus' anointing,[12] and one is a messianic quotation from the Psalms.[13] The remaining reference claims God's anointing upon all the recipients of Paul's letter,[14] as do the only two references to the noun *chrisma*—anointing—in John's letter.[15] However, two factors suggest a wider application of the idea of anointing than the few occurrences

---

[1] Judges 6:34; 11:29; 13:25; 14:6, 19; 15:14.
[2] Saul anointed, 1 Samuel 10:1; David anointed, 1 Samuel 16:13. Note that in both cases the anointing was accompanied by the Spirit coming upon them in power.
[3] Both the High Priest, Exodus 29:7, and other priests, Exodus 30:30.
[4] Balaam, Numbers 23:5; 24:2; Elisha, 1 Kings 19:16. The anointing of Elijah is also implicit in 2 Kings 2:9; and in the activity of the Spirit in Ezekiel 2:2; 3:12, etc.
[5] R. Lairds Harris et al., eds., *Theological Wordbook of the Old Testament*. (Chicago IL: Moody Press, 1980), 530
[6] Note both Saul and David's call to account for their sin on the basis of the Lord's anointing, 1 Samuel 15:17 and 2 Samuel 12:7.
[7] 1 Samuel 26:9–11.
[8] Saul, 1 Samuel 10:1; David, 1 Samuel 16:13.
[9] Isaiah 9:1–7; 11:1–5; 61:1.
[10] Numbers 11:16–17, 24–25.
[11] 2 Kings 2:9 and 15.
[12] Luke 4:18; Acts 4:27; 10:38.
[13] Hebrews 1:9.
[14] 2 Corinthians 1:21.
[15] 1 John 2:20 and 27.

suggest. The first is found in the New Testament emphasis of naming Jesus the Christ, *Christos*—the Anointed One. It was this anointing which not only set him apart for his specific work, but also which provided the source of his power for the work.[1] This is significant for his followers, for as Forbes points out, ". . . they were not called Jesusians, but Christians—like the Anointed One, they were 'anointed ones.'"[2]

The second factor is the widely recorded activity of the Holy Spirit in the New Testament which parallels the anointing of the Spirit in the Old. The separating and empowering motifs of the Old Testament are clearly documented in the New.[3] Thus the New Testament work of the Holy Spirit was a continuation of his work in the Old, but with one significant difference: his Spirit was poured out on "all flesh"[4] and not reserved for a select few; the anointing for service was now available for whatever work to which God has called the individual or community.

In reviewing the paradigm of the Spirit's activity in Jesus' life, we note the Holy Spirit coming upon him at baptism,[5] impelling Jesus into the place of temptation at a time when he was "full of the Holy Spirit";[6] his triumphant return "in the power of the Spirit"[7] and his anointing by the Spirit for the preaching of the Gospel.[8] The four gospel writers all agreed that it was this Spirit empowered Jesus who would eventually baptize his followers with the Holy Spirit,[9] and the coming of the Spirit on the day of Pentecost was seen as that fulfilment.[10] Thus empowering for service is implicit in the anointing work of the Spirit.

---

[1] Luke 4:18–19.
[2] Forbes, *The Holy Spirit and Preaching*, 45.
[3] Acts 1:8 is the basis of the power of the New Testament church.
[4] The fulfilment of Joel 2:28–32 in Acts 2:16–21.
[5] Luke 3:21.
[6] Luke 4:1.
[7] Luke 4:14.
[8] Luke 4:18–19.
[9] Matthew 3:11; Mark 1:8; Luke 3:16; John 1:33.
[10] Acts 1:4–5; 11:15–17.

Bryan Norford

## APPENDIX 2

### NEW TESTAMENT VIEW OF THE HOLY SPIRIT AS COMMUNICATOR

Scripture recognizes the work of the Holy Spirit as author of the Old Testament, and as teacher/illuminator of the young Church in the New Testament. As such, the Spirit also provides special words or help at times of crisis or importance and is a continuing conveyor of God's message of salvation—the Gospel or Good News to the world. The primary example of the Holy Spirit as conveyor of truth came through Jesus Christ himself, both by example and teaching, and most categories of the Spirit's work in this area are attested to by Jesus, before witness to it by his supporters as the following indicates.

Jesus recognizes the Spirit's authorship of the Old Testament in the inspiration of David by the Holy Spirit for Psalm 110.[1] Luke Luke follows this by identifying the authorship of the Holy Spirit in Isaiah,[2] Psalms,[3] David as a specific author,[4] and the writer to Hebrews similarly regards Jeremiah.[5] The generality of the authorship is attested to by specific declarations that all prophecy

---

[1] Mark 12:36.
[2] Acts 28:25.
[3] Acts 4:25, Hebrews 3:7.
[4] Acts 1:16.
[5] Hebrews 10:15.

was given by the Holy Spirit[1] and that all Scripture is "God-breathed"[2]—an implicit reference to the Holy Spirit.

Jesus also taught that the Holy Spirit's work brings conviction and illumination to men,[3] and demonstrated it by his instruction to the apostles through the Holy Spirit.[4] Later we find the Church strengthened and encouraged by the Holy Spirit following its persecution[5] and enlightened by the Holy Spirit.[6] The reception of of the word occasioned joy of the Holy Spirit[7] and rejection of that that word was a considered a rejection of God the Holy Spirit.[8]

The Holy Spirit provided specific direction in times of crisis or importance. This is demonstrated at a critical time in Jesus' life when he was driven by the Spirit into a time of temptation.[9] It is reasonable to believe that the Spirit who led Jesus into the path of temptation, was also the one providing illumination during it. Nothing so drastic is recorded of others, but many instances of succour and special direction are both taught and recorded. The coming of the Messiah was revealed to Zechariah[10] and Simeon.[11] Jesus himself indicated that the Holy Spirit would provide direction under persecution,[12] and the disciples experienced it.[13] Paul was sent on his missionary journeys,[14] discerned opposition,[15] was directed on his journey,[16] and warned of prison to come[17] all

---

[1] 2 Peter 1:21.
[2] 2 Timothy 3:16.
[3] John 14:26, 16:5–15.
[4] Acts 1:2.
[5] Acts 9:31.
[6] Hebrews 6:4, cf. also 9:8.
[7] 1 Thessalonians 1:5–6.
[8] 1 Thessalonians 4:8.
[9] Mark 1:12.
[10] Luke 1:67.
[11] Luke 2:25–26.
[12] Matthew 10:19, Mark 13:11, Luke 12:12.
[13] Acts 4:8–12.
[14] Acts 13:2.
[15] Acts 13:9.
[16] Acts 16:6.
[17] Acts 20:23, 21:11.

## Anointed Preaching

by the Holy Spirit in those formative days of a vulnerable Church. The Holy Spirit gave guidance in conference at the Jerusalem Council,[1] and was regarded as the guardian of the truth of the Gospel.[2]

For our purpose, the focal body of information about the Spirit as conveyor of truth is contained in the references to preaching. Luke, the foremost interpreter of the work of the Spirit among the Gospel writers, gives witness to the Spirit's work in the life of Jesus for the carrying out of his ministry. In addition to his Spirit-commissioning mentioned above, the Holy Spirit descended on him at his baptism,[3] He went into his ministry "full of the Holy Spirit,"[4] and experienced the joy of the Spirit at a preview of its completion.[5]

But Jesus was not content to experience the Holy Spirit in his own proclamation, but saw the Spirit as essential to the ministry of his disciples. The sending of the Holy Spirit was not only to teach and remind the disciples of his sayings,[6] but also to convict their hearers.[7] Further, he himself taught the disciples by the Holy Spirit,[8] and instructed them to await their own enduement by the Holy Spirit as a necessary prerequisite to their witness of him.[9] That this enduement was necessary was not only taught by Jesus, but also experienced in the changed demeanour of the disciples on the Day of Pentecost. That the enduement was for witness was attested by the basis of their overall message,[10] and the content of

---

[1] Acts 15:28.
[2] 2 Timothy 1:14.
[3] Luke 3:22.
[4] Luke 4:1.
[5] Luke 10:18–21.
[6] John 14:26, 16:12–15.
[7] John 16:8–11.
[8] Acts 1:2.
[9] Acts 1:4–8.
[10] Acts 2:11.

Peter's sermon that day.[1] Peter's own testimony was that those who who preached the Gospel did so by the Holy Spirit.[2]

Those who followed witnessed to the same Holy Spirit as the source of their preaching. Even Paul admitted his own weakness, fear and inadequate speaking skills. He credited the Holy Spirit with forming the Gospel in his hearers hearts,[3] so that the basis of their faith would be legitimate.[4] There could never be communication from God to man without the Holy Spirit.[5] The conviction of the deity of Christ was from the Holy Spirit,[6] the testimony of signs came from him;[7] even the burden for the lost, for both Jews[8] and Gentiles.[9]

---

[1] Acts 2:14–39.
[2] 1 Peter 1:12.
[3] 1 Corinthians 2:1–4, 1 Thessalonians 1:5.
[4] 1 Corinthians 1:5.
[5] 1 Corinthians 2:6–16.
[6] 1 Corinthians 12:3.
[7] Hebrews 2:4.
[8] Romans 9:1–4.
[9] Romans 15:16.

## APPENDIX 3

### THE NECESSITY OF WEAKNESS IN THE NEW TESTAMENT

The need of human weakness through which the power of God is displayed, is a major theme in the New Testament. This appendix is not exhaustive, many other texts and nuances may come to mind, but it will show the pervasiveness of the theme. Jesus himself is the first paradigm clearly displayed in the Servant passages of Isaiah (whether these eventually refer to Jesus, the theme remains regarding God's Servant).[1] His vulnerability is seen in his natural birth and dependence on others for life as a baby[2] and and protection from those seeking the child's life.[3] He was subject to temptation;[4] became hungry[5] and tired,[6] and had no place of his his own.[7] He was betrayed[8] and denied,[9] and subjected himself to to the pain and death of the cross.[10]

---

[1] Isaiah 50:6–9; 52:14; 53:1–3, 7–12.
[2] Luke 2:7
[3] Matthew 2:13–14.
[4] Matthew 4:1–11.
[5] Matthew 4:2.
[6] Mark 4:38; John 4:6.
[7] Matthew 8:20.
[8] Matthew 26:14–16.
[9] Matthew 26:69–75.
[10] Philippians 2:5–8. Note that this passage raises a related issue, that of the link between suffering and glory, cf. v. 9, at "Therefore," Other Scriptures: Romans 8:17–18; 2 Corinthians 4:17; Philippians 3:10; 2 Timothy 2:12.

Jesus' teaching also revealed the same theme regarding those who would follow him; the weak and inadequate[1] and the persecuted[2] would be blessed. He came for the sinners, not the righteous.[3] The "first would be last"[4] and the price of authority was was servanthood.[5] To understand him[6] and enter heaven[7] required required childlikeness. His servants would be "sheep among wolves,"[8] and their joy should rest in acceptance into heaven, not their power.[9] Like Jesus, their reward was in denial of themselves.[10]

In the letters, Paul majors on this theme to the Corinthian Church, who had clearly missed this aspect of the Christian faith. God had entrusted his message to the "foolishness of preaching";[11] to the foolish, weak and lowly to deny human pride.[12] Paul placed himself in this category,[13] and revealed his own weakness to show up the Corinthian error the more clearly.[14] He denied himself remuneration for their sake;[15] his distress was for their sake,[16] and he rejoiced in the suffering he endured, for it enabled the power of God to be seen more clearly through him.[17] This enabled him to be completely open to them—both strengths and weaknesses.[18] Paul considered personal boldness as a standard of the world and

---

[1] Matthew 5:1–6.
[2] Matthew 5:10–12.
[3] Matthew 9:13.
[4] Mark 9:35.
[5] Matthew 20:26–28.
[6] Matthew 11:25–26.
[7] Matthew 18:3–4.
[8] Matthew 10:16.
[9] Luke 10:19–20.
[10] Matthew 10:37–39; 19:27–30.
[11] 1 Corinthians 1:21.
[12] 1 Corinthians 1:27–29.
[13] 1 Corinthians 2:1–5.
[14] 1 Corinthians 4:6–16.
[15] 1 Corinthians 9:12–18.
[16] 2 Corinthians 1:3–7.
[17] 2 Corinthians 1:8–9; 4:7–12.
[18] 2 Corinthians 6:3–10.

## Anointed Preaching

rejected it as a weapon in order to give place to divine power.[1] As he nears the end of his second letter, it becomes clear that the Corinthians completely misconstrued his humility and servanthood for weakness.[2] Contrary to his conviction, he "boasts" about himself using his readers categories, but will only boast about his weakness, for it is in his weakness that he receives God's strength.[3] strength.[3]

As is to be expected, the theme taught in the preceding Scriptures, is also experienced in the growth of the fledgling Church in Acts. The incidents are numerous; the major ones will be sufficiently representative. Obvious and frequently cited was the change in the demeanour of the disciples on the Day of Pentecost compared with their fearfulness following the crucifixion.[4] For Peter it was clear that the power he had was not his,[5] and critics recognized the same.[6] Stephen's articulate speech was from the Spirit[7] and his witness to the Jews was in great personal danger and death.[8] Peter[9] and later Paul and Silas,[10] escaped from prison at a time of their weakness. While in Corinth, God, not circumstances, guaranteed Paul's protection.[11] Paul's arrest in Jerusalem was not a failure of God's protection but rather a means of taking the gospel to Rome[12]

---

[1] 2 Corinthians 10:1–5.
[2] The whole passage 2 Corinthians 11:1–12:13 needs to be read to convey the burden of Paul's argument, but note verses 4–7.
[3] 2 Corinthians 12:1–10. Too much time has been spent on Paul's "thorn"! It is personal weakness as a vehicle for God's power that is the point of this passage.
[4] John 20:19; cf. Acts 2:4–5, and their various subsequent appearances on charges of preaching the Gospel.
[5] Acts 3:6.
[6] Acts 4:13.
[7] Acts 6:8–10.
[8] Acts 7:51–60.
[9] Acts 12:7.
[10] Acts 16:25–26.
[11] Acts 18:9–11.
[12] Acts, chapters 21 to 28.

Bryan Norford

# APPENDIX 4

## SOME OUTLINES OF PENTECOSTAL SERMONS

The following sermon outlines have been taken from *Preparation for Preaching* compiled by Louis H. Hauff. There is no publisher printed in the book, but it dates from about 1967, and is obtainable from the Central Bible College Library, Springfield, Missouri. The sermons contained in the book are by well-known preachers of good standing in the North American Pentecostal movement, and those selected have been chosen as far as possible to be typical of Pentecostal preaching.

The sermons chosen convey variety and are commented on in the text of this book. Also, it must be realized that the written word can only convey a portion of what would be considered as "anointed preaching." Note also, that Bible references used in the sermons may be from different translations than the NIV generally used in this book

Bryan Norford

Anointed Preaching

## A TIGHT SQUEEZE by C. M. Ward
(See page 66)

**Text:**

> And the angel of the Lord stood in the way for an adversary against him . . . in a narrow place, where there was no way to turn, either to the right hand or to the left
>
> Numbers 22:24, 26.

**Introduction:**
This is the story of a man who tried his best to avoid a confrontation with God. He wanted God to come to terms with him. He thought God was denying him something, He could not see that he was involved with the world's welfare and the salvation of mankind. *A man in this condition doesn't have the sense of an animal.*

**Body of the Message:**
Here are some of the "narrow places" in which you may suddenly find yourself:

**1. The Narrow Place of Sickness**
A sick bed or hospital room is a very narrow place. Sickness makes you look at yourself (Psalm 75:7).

**2. The Narrow Place of Temptation**
Temptation *forces decision.*

You are either a liar or you are not a liar. You are either dishonest or honest. Temptation is hand-to-hand combat. Life has a way of asking for a conclusion.

### 3. The Narrow Place of Death
You can no longer avoid God in that moment, *the final moment of truth*. "Another shall gird thee, and carry thee whither thou wouldest not." (John 21:18).
Sin never looks good at a deathbed.

**Application or Invitation:**
Your fortunes are "narrowing" sinner. You can't make a deal with God. You are heading toward the point of no return. *God is closing in on you.* God wants to save you if he can.

## WHERE DO YOU GO FROM WIT'S END? by C. M. Ward
(See page 66)

**Text:**

> *They reel to and fro, and stagger like a drunken man, and are at their wit's end*
> *(Psalm 107:27).*

**Introduction:**

This junction is on everyone's travel schedule. It is a moment when you have exhausted every means at hand and do not know what's next. It is best described in verses 27 and 28. There are many different kinds of storms. You may be caught in one tomorrow. What should you do? To whom should you turn?

**1. The Situation** (verses 23 through 27).
What does it mean to be at wit's end?
Illustrations—Moses, Exodus 15:24; Hannah, 1 Samuel 1:6, 10 and 20; Elisha, 2 Kings 4:32–33; Hezekiah, 2 Kings 19:14 and 15; Paul, Acts 16:25.

**2. The Remedy** (verse 28)
What preciptates this? *"Then* They cry unto the Lord."
Look at the conjunction, *"and* He bringeth them out of their distresses." You need God *and* God is waiting for you.
    a) He made a great *calm*, Mark 4:39 and Isaiah 26:3.
    b) He gave them great *gladness*. Gladness and quietness go together, Romans 14:17.

c) He brought them *safely* home, He bringeth them unto their desired haven, Psalm 37:5; Acts 12:5.

**Application or Invitation:**
What he did for Peter in prison, when it seemed to be an absolutely hopeless situation, *he can do for you, and is willing to do for you.* Turn to God. He will not fail you.

**THE SONG OF SALVATION By G. Raymond Carlson**
(See page 66)

**Scripture Passage:** Ephesians 1:3–14

**Introduction:**
In Ephesians, Paul reaches the greatest breadth, highest heights, and deepest depths of inspiration as he contemplates the position and standing of the Church. He states that the Church is God's "workmanship" (2:10), which means literally, "masterwork" or "masterpiece." The Greek word used is *poiama* from which we get our word "poem". It is used in only one other place (Romans 1:20). There reference is made to God's word in creation of the natural world. In Ephesians, he refers to his "masterpiece", the Church.

This passage—the Magna Charta of Christianity—outlines the plan of salvation from before time (verse 4) to beyond time (verse 10). It describes the united effort of the Triune God in bringing redemption. The expression, "in Christ," a favourite with Paul, occurs eleven times.

This poem has three stanzas which combine into a great hymn of praise. The entire passage, a total of 268 words, has only three sentences, each a stanza presenting redemption as planned by the Father, provided by the Son, and wrought by the Holy Spirit.

**1. God The Father Planned Redemption for Us.**
In tribute to the Father, three of his acts on our behalf are mentioned:

**A. He Chose Us** (verse 4).
This relates to election. The word for "chosen" in the Greek text means "to pick out, choose." It occurs 21 times in the New Testament and is translated "choose". The adjective derived from this word occurs 23 times, and is translated "elect" 16 times and "chosen" 7 times. Election is:
1. According to the foreknowledge of God (1 Peter 1:2, Ephesians. 1:4–6)
2. According to the faith of the heart (Titus 1:1)
3. According to the fruit of the life (2 Peter 1:10).

**B. He Adopted Us** (verse 5)
This word—peculiar to Paul—occurs 3 times in Romans (8:15 and 23; 9:14), once in Galatians (4:5), and here in Ephesians. Literally it means "placing as a son." Walking in full victory of this position is a life in the Spirit.
Sonship is:
1. Declared (Galatians 4:1–5).
2. Defined (Galatians 4:6 and 7; Ephesians 1:5 and 6).
3. Desirable (Romans 8:14–17).
4. Demonstrated (Romans 8:14 and 15; Galatians 4:6).

**C. He Accepted Us** (verse 6).
We are made "accepted"—not "acceptable"—in the Beloved. The bulk of the last half of the verse is one word in the original text and is found in only one other place in the New Testament, Luke 1:28: "thou that art highly favoured."

**2. God The Son Provided Redemption in Us.**
In tribute to the Son, three of his acts on our behalf are mentioned:

### A. He Redeemed Us (verse 7)
1. The promise of redemption was
    (a) Planned in eternity (1 Peter. 1:18–20; Revelation 13:8).
    (b) Promised in Eden (Genesis. 3:15).
2. The price of redemption was
    (a) Pictured by the Kinsman-Redeemer (Levitcus 25:47–49).
    (b) Purchased by Calvary's blood (1 Peter 1:18,19).
3. The provision of redemption was a
    (a) Pre-eminent need met (Matthew 20:28; 1 Corinthians 6:20).
    (b) Perfect salvation provided (Ephesians 1:7).

### B. He Makes Known Unto Us the Mystery of His Will (verse 9).
1. The gospel is called the mystery of God's will.
2. God's purpose—(marginal reading of Acts 15:14–16).
3. Phillip's translation of verse 9.

### C. He Grants Us an Inheritance (verse 11).
1. Circle "we"—we are promised a share in all things which will one day belong to Christ.
2. Word has a dual aspect. We have a heritage, and we are his heritage.
3. He has a tremendous stake—purchased at awful cost—in us.

## 3. God The Holy Spirit Has Given Us:

### A. A Seal (verse 13). Describe the seal as used in ancient days. Compare to the notarial seal today.

### B. An Earnest (verse 14). Illustrate from the commercial world. It indicates a down payment to insure fulfilment of a negotiation.

**C. A Pledge** (verse 14). A promise that more will follow. It can be likened to the engagement ring.

## Conclusion

All three stanzas—each a sentence—have expressed a triumphant tribute to the Father, Son, and Holy Ghost. Each presents the part each person played. Now note each stanza ends with the same expression, "to the praise of his glory" (verses 6, 12 and 14). All God's purposes centre in himself. His actions find birth in his will. His purposes and his acts are for his own glory.

God's highest purpose will find fulfilment in the Church. When the Church is manifested in glory at the completion of redemption, Christ "shall see of the travail of his soul, and shall be satisfied" (Isaiah 53:11), and the Father shall satisfy his eternal purpose "to the praise of His glory". Conclude with Romans 11:33.

## THE WHITE ELEPHANT by Louis H. Hauff
(See page 67)

An expressive idiom of the English language has come to us from the little country of Siam. It stems from a strange custom. Whenever the King of Siam wished to ruin any of his courtiers, he would present him with a white elephant. Inasmuch as such animals are sacred in that land, it was impossible for the man to do away with the elephant. There was no way for him to get rid of the unusual beast unless the king or high priest took it off his hands. The expense of keeping such an animal was enormous and eventually ruined the courtier. From that custom we have come to call a "white elephant" any item that is unusable or that is expensive to keep and of no value. Sin is like that white elephant. Here are five points to illustrate the similarity:

### The White Elephant of Sin is in Man's Possession Through No Fault of His Own.

"All have sinned, and come short of the glory of God" (Romans 3:23). "There is no man that sinneth not" (I Kings 8:46). The Bible does not try to prove that we have sin. That is taken for granted, for sin is the curse of mankind. Sin entered through our first parents, Adam and Eve, and has been passed on to all generations. David said, "I was shapen in iniquity and in sin did my mother conceive me" (Psalm 51:5). Though sin is in us through no fault of our own, we are guilty if we continue to sin.

**Man Cannot Get Rid of This White Elephant by His Own Efforts.**
We cannot remove sin in our own strength. It does no good to reform, make New Year's resolutions, or turn over a new leaf. We do not need just a new leaf; we need a whole new book. The heathen throughout the world are trying all forms of penance and self-punishment, but to no avail. "By grace are ye saved through faith; and that not of yourselves: it is the gift of God; Not of works, lest any man should boast" (Ephesians 2:8–9). "Not by works of righteousness which we have done, but according to His mercy he saved us . . ." (Titus 3:5).

**A White Elephant is Costly to Keep.**
"The way of transgressors is hard" (Proverbs 13:15). When one buys a new car, he receives a book of instructions and rules. If he takes care of the car according to the rules, it will render him good service. If he goes contrary to the rules, the upkeep on the car will be expensive. Sin is costly to man, for the sinner is living contrary to the law of God. If men do not obey God's rules, it costs them—mentally, physically, and spiritually. Sin shuts men out from God. "Your sins have hid his face from you" (Isaiah 59:2).

**A White Elephant Means Eventual Ruin.**
"The wages of sin is death" (Romans 6:23). "The soul that sinneth, it shall die" (Ezekiel 18:4). "He that soweth to his flesh shall of the flesh reap corruption" (Galatians 6:8). God has a penitentiary for all that sin, even as we have places of confinement for evildoers. Sin will bring not just life imprisonment, but eternal life imprisonment. "Them that know not God, and that obey not the gospel of our Lord Jesus Christ: Who shall be punished with everlasting destruction from the presence of the Lord" (2 Thessalonians 1:8–9). This doom will come upon those who hold on to sin and refuse to be saved from it. The fault is not God's, but the sinner's.

**Only the King or High Priest Can Remove the White Elephant.** Jesus Christ is King of kings and Lord of lords, who can free man from sin. "If we confess our sins, he is faithful and just to forgive us our sins, and to cleanse us from all unrighteousness" (I John 1:9). "Behold the lamb of God, which taketh away the sin of the world" (John 1:29).

Jesus Christ is also our High Priest. "By his own blood he entered in once into the holy place, having obtained eternal redemption for us" (Hebrews 9:12). "Seeing then that we have a great high priest, that is passed into the heavens, Jesus the Son of God . . . Let us therefore come boldly unto the throne of grace, that we may obtain mercy, and find grace to help in time of need" (Hebrews 4:14 and 16).

No one need have on his hands sin and its consequences. Our Lord Jesus Christ stands ready to set men free from sin and give eternal life.

Bryan Norford

# BIBLIOGRAPHY

Allen, Roland. *The Spontaneous Expansion of the Church.* Grand Rapids, MI: Eerdmans, 1962.

Baumann, Daniel J. *An Introduction to Contempary Preaching.* Grand Rapids MI: Baker Book House, 1972.

Berkhof, Hendrikus. *The Doctrine of the Holy Spirit.* London: The Epworth Press, undated.

Brown, Colin. *Miracles and the Critical Mind.* Grand Rapids MI: Eerdmans, 1984.

Brown, Francis, and S. R. Driver, Charles. A. Briggs, C. A. *A Hebrew and English Lexicon of the Old Testament.* Oxford: Clarendon Press, 1980

Bruce, F. F. *The Books and the Parchments.* Old Tappan NJ: Fleming H. Revell Co., 3rd edition, 1963.

Bruner, Frederic Dale. *A Theology of the Holy Spirit.* Grand Rapids MI: Eerdmans, 1970.

Burge, Gary M. *The Anointed Community: The Holy Spirit in the Gospel of John.* Grand Rapids MI: Eerdmans, 1987.

Byrd, Joseph Kendall. *Formulation of a Classical Pentecostal Homiletic in Dialogue with Contemporary Protestant Homiletics.* Ph.D. dissertation, Southern Baptist Theological Seminary, 1990.

Douglas, L. D. *The New Bible Dictionary.* Grand Rapids, Michigan IL: Eerdmans, 1962

Duffield, Guy P. Jr. *Pentecostal Preaching*. New York NY: Vantage Press, c. 1956.

Ervin, Howard M. "Hermeneutics: A Pentecostal Option," *Essays on Apostolic Themes*, ed., Paul Elbert. Peabody MA: Hendrickson, 1985.

Fee, Gordon D. and Douglas Stuart. *Gospel and Spirit: Issues in New Testament Hermeneutics*. Peabody MA: Hendrickson, 1991.

_____. *How to Read the Bible For All Its Worth*. Grand Rapids MI: Zondervan, 1982.

_____. *The First Epistle to the Corinthians*. Grand Rapids MI: Eerdmans, 1987.

Forbes, James. *The Holy Spirit and Preaching*. Nashville TN: Abingdon Press, 1989.

Ford, D. W. Cleverley. *The Ministry of the Word*. Grand Rapids MI: Eerdmans, 1979.

Gee, Donald. *Spiritual Gifts in the Work of the Ministry Today*. Springfield MO: Gospel Publishing House, 1963.

Gunkel, Hermann. *The Influence of the Holy Spirit, the Popular View of the Apostolic Age and the Teaching of the Apostle Paul*. tr. Roy A. Harrisville and Philip A. Quanbeck II. Philadelphia PN: Fortress Press, 1979.

Harris, R. Laird, ed. *Theological Wordbook of the Old Testament*. Chicago IL: Moody Press, 1980.

Hiebert, Paul G. "Discerning the Work of God," *Charismatic Experiences in History*, ed., Cecil N. Robeck. Peabody MA: Hendrickson, 1985.

Horton, Harold. *Preaching and Homiletics*. Luton, Bedfordshire, UK: Assemblies of God Publishing House, 1946.

Hughes, Ray H. *Pentecostal Preaching.* Cleveland TN: Pathway Press, 1981.

Keys, Leland R. "One Man's Methods," *Preparation for Preaching,* compiler Loius H. Hauff. Available from the Central Bible College Library, Springfield MI.

Lloyd-Jones, D. Martyn. *Preaching and Preachers.* Grand Rapids MI: Zondervan Publishing House, 1971.

_____. *Revival.* Westchester IL: Crossway Books, 1987.

Longenecker, Richard. *Biblical Exegesis in the Apostolic Period.* Grand Rapids MI: Eerdmans, 1975.

_____. "Can We Reproduce the Exegesis of the New Testament?" *Tyndale Bulletin,* 21, 1970.

Marcel, Pierre. *The Relevance of Preaching,* Tr. Rob Roy McGregor. Grand Rapids MI: Baker Book House, 1963.

Massey, James Earl. *The Sermon in Perspective.* Grand Rapids MI: Baker Book House, 1976.

McConnell Don R. *A Different Gospel.* Peabody, MA: Hendrickson, 1995

Menzies, William W. "The Methodology of Pentecostal Theology: An Essay on Hermeneutics," *Essays on Apostolic Themes*, ed. Paul Elbert. Peabody MA: Hendrickson, 1985.

Miller, Thomas W. "O Foolish Pentecostals," *The Pentecostal Testimony*, October 1991.

Moon Jesse K. "The Holy Spirit in Preaching," *Paraclete* 11, Fall 1977, 26.

Oates, Wayne. *The Holy Spirit in Five Worlds.* New York NY: Association Press, 1968.

Piper, John. *The Supremacy of God in Preaching.* Grand Rapids MI: Baker Book House, 1990.

Ramm, Bernard. *Protestant Biblical Interpretation*. Grand Rapids MI: Baker Book House, 1970.

Reid, Ron. "Academic or Anointed?" *The Pentecostal Testimony*, January 1986.

Smalley, Gary E. "Anticipating Not a Decade of Disaster, But . . ." *The Pentecostal Testimony*, March 1990.

Spurgeon, Charles Haddon. "The Holy Spirit and the Ministry of Preaching." *Theories of Preaching, Selected Readings in the Homiletical Tradition*, ed., Richard Lischer. Durham NC: The Labrinth Press, 1987.

Stott, John R. W. *Baptism and Fulness: The Work of the Holy Spirit Today*, 2nd edition. London: Intervarsity Press, 1975.

_____. *Between Two Worlds, The Art of Preaching in the Twentieth Century*. Grand Rapids, MI: Eerdmans, 1982.

Stronstad, Roger. "Pentecostal Experience and Hermeneutics," *Paraclete* 26:1, Winter 1992.

_____. *The Charismatic Theology of St. Luke*. Peabody MA: Hendrickson, 1984.

_____. "Trends in Pentecostal Hermeneutics," *Paraclete*, 22:3, Summer 1988.

Sweazey, George E. *Preaching the Good News*. Englewood Cliffs NJ: Prentice-Hall Inc., 1976.

Walker, Williston. *A History of the Christian Church*. New York NY: Charles Scribner's Sons, 3rd edition 1970).

Woods, Roger. "Preach the Word," *Resource*, 5:2, November-December, 1990.

## ABOUT THE AUTHOR

The author, Bryan Norford, grew up in the UK, making architecture his first profession. With his wife Ann and young family, he immigrated to Canada in 1965 where he continued his architectural profession.

He obtained a Master of Divinity degree at Regent College, Vancouver in 1982. He then pastored churches and taught in Bible colleges for several years in the lower mainland where he published a series of study guides on apologetics, ethics, and Bible surveys.

He is now retired and living in Lethbridge, Alberta where he and Ann authored their first book, *Happy Together: Daily Insights for Families from Scripture,* published in 2009. Bryan authored further books, *Guess Who's Coming to Reign! Jesus Talks about His Return*, in 2010 and *Gone with the Spirit: Tracking the Holy Spirit through the Bible*, in 2011, and continues to write.

Further materials are on his website at www.norfords-writings.com.

Ann and Bryan enjoy their writing activities, and spending time with their expanding family of grandchildren and great grandchildren